MACMILLAN M_____S

General Ed_____

MACMILLAN MODERN NOVELISTS

Published titles

E. M. FORSTER Norman Page
WILLIAM GOLDING James Gindin
MARCEL PROUST Philip Thody
SIX WOMEN NOVELISTS Merryn Williams
JOHN UPDIKE Judie Newman
H. G. WELLS Michael Draper

Forthcoming titles

ALBERT CAMUS Philip Thody
JOSEPH CONRAD Owen Knowles
FYODOR DOSTOEVSKY Peter Conradi
WILLIAM FAULKNER David Dowling
F. SCOTT FITZGERALD John S. Whitley
GUSTAVE FLAUBERT David Roe
JOHN FOWLES Simon Gatrell
GRAHAM GREENE Neil McEwan
HENRY JAMES Alan Bellringer
JAMES JOYCE Richard Brown
D. H. LAWRENCE G. M. Hyde
DORIS LESSING Ruth Whittaker
MALCOLM LOWRY Tony Bareham
GEORGE ORWELL Valerie Meyers
BARBARA PYM Michael Cotsell
MURIEL SPARK Norman Page
GERTRUDE STEIN Shirley Neuman
EVELYN WAUGH Jacqueline McDonnell
VIRGINIA WOOLF Edward Bishop

Series Standing Order

If you would like to receive future titles in this series as they are
published, you can make use of our standing order facility. To place a
standing order please contact your bookseller or, in case of difficulty,
write to us at the address below with your name and address and the
name of the series. Please state with which title you wish to begin your
standing order. (If you live outside the United Kingdom we may not
have the rights for your area, in which case we will forward your order
to the publisher concerned.)

Customer Services Department, Macmillan Distribution Ltd
Houndmills, Basingstoke, Hampshire, RG21 2XS, England.

MACMILLAN MODERN NOVELISTS
JOHN UPDIKE

Judie Newman

**MACMILLAN
EDUCATION**

First published 1988

Published by
Higher and Further Education Division
MACMILLAN PUBLISHERS LTD
Houndmills, Basingstoke, Hampshire RG21 2XS
and London
Companies and representatives
throughout the world

Typeset by Wessex Typesetters
(Division of The Eastern Press Ltd)
Frome, Somerset

Printed in Hong Kong

British Library Cataloguing in Publication Data
Newman, Judie
  John Updike.—(Macmillan modern novelists).
  1. Updike, John—Criticism and
  interpretation
  I. Title
  813'.54   PS3571.P4Z/
  ISBN 0–333–40690–7
  ISBN 0–333–40691–5 Pbk

Contents

Acknowledgments

The author and publishers wish to thank the following publishers for permission to quote from the works of John Updike: Alfred A. Knopf, Inc. and André Deutsch Ltd. for extracts from *The Poorhouse Fair* (US copyright 1959 by John Updike), *Rabbit, Run* (US copyright 1960, 1964 by John Updike), *The Centaur* (US copyright 1962, 1963 by John Updike), *Of the Farm* (US copyright 1965 by John Updike), *Couples* (US copyright 1968 by John Updike), *Rabbit Redux* (US copyright 1971 by John Updike), *A Month of Sundays* (US copyright 1974, 1975 by John Updike), *Marry Me: A Romance* (US copyright 1971, 1973, 1976 by John Updike), *The Coup* (US copyright 1978 by John Updike), *Rabbit Is Rich* (US copyright 1981 by John Updike), *The Witches of Eastwick* (US copyright 1984 by John Updike) and *Roger's Version* (US copyright 1986 by John Updike). I gratefully acknowledge the financial assistance of the Small Grants Sub-Committee of the University of Newcastle upon Tyne, which enabled me to undertake research in other libraries. Special thanks are also due to the staff of the National Library of Scotland, and the Library of the University of Newcastle upon Tyne, in particular the staff of the Inter-Library Loans Department for speedy and efficient assistance in obtaining bibliographical material. Alison Gallagher, Kathleen O'Rawe and Margaret Jones provided equally efficient secretarial assistance. I acknowledge a general debt to my colleagues and students in Newcastle, who helped me to define my ideas, and a special debt to Halla Beloff, Hermann Moisl and Linda Anderson for invaluable information and advice. Finally I should like to thank Ian, Christopher and Ivy Revie who all gave generously of their time, energy and moral support. This book is dedicated to my parents, Alice and Cash Newman, with gratitude for a childhood spent in that 'magical margin' which John Updike celebrates in 'Macbech'.

General Editor's Preface

The death of the novel has often been announced, and part of the secret of its obstinate vitality must be its capacity for growth, adaptation, self-renewal and even self-transformation: like some vigorous organism in a speeded-up Darwinian ecosystem, it adapts itself quickly to a changing world. War and revolution, economic crisis and social change, radically new ideologies such as Marxism and Freudianism, have made this century unprecedented in human history in the speed and extent of change, but the novel has shown an extraordinary capacity to find new forms and techniques and to accommodate new ideas and conceptions of human nature and human experience, and even to take up new positions on the nature of fiction itself.

In the generations immediately preceding and following 1914, the novel underwent a radical redefinition of its nature and possibilities. The present series of monographs is devoted to the novelists who created the modern novel and to those who, in their turn, either continued and extended, or reacted against and rejected, the traditions established during that period of intense exploration and experiment. It includes a number of those who lived and wrote in the nineteenth century but whose innovative contribution to the art of fiction makes it impossible to ignore them in any account of the origins of the modern novel; it also includes the so-called 'modernists' and those who in the mid- and late twentieth century have emerged as outstanding practitioners of this genre. The scope is, inevitably, international; not only, in the migratory and exile-haunted world of our century, do writers refuse to heed national frontiers – 'English' literature lays claim to Conrad the Pole, Henry James the American, and Joyce the Irishman – but geniuses such as Flaubert, Dostoevsky and Kafka have had an influence on the fiction of many nations.

Each volume in the series is intended to provide an introduction to the fiction of the writer concerned, both for those approaching him or her for the first time and for those who are already familiar with some parts of the achievement in question and now wish to place it in the context of the total *oeuvre*. Although essential information relating to the writer's life and times is given, usually in an opening chapter, the approach is primarily critical and the emphasis is not upon 'background' or generalisations but upon close examination of important texts. Where an author is notably prolific, major texts have been selected for detailed attention but an attempt has also been made to convey, more summarily, a sense of the nature and quality of the author's work as a whole. Those who want to read further will find suggestions in the select bibliography included in each volume. Many novelists are, of course, not only novelists but also poets, essayists, biographers, dramatists, travel writers and so forth; many have practised shorter forms of fiction; and many have written letters or kept diaries that constitute a significant part of their literary output. A brief study cannot hope to deal with all these in detail, but where the shorter fiction and the non-fictional writings, public and private, have an important relationship to the novels, some space has been devoted to them.

NORMAN PAGE

1
Introduction

As a glance at a bibliography reveals, John Updike is an extremely prolific writer, whose published work includes 12 novels, 9 collections of short stories, 17 volumes of verse, 3 bulky anthologies of non-fictional prose, children's books, journalism and a mass of minor items. None the less, the prime charge levelled against Updike by his criticis is that he is 'a writer who has very little to say' (Norman Podhoretz).[1] Though Podhoretz's comment is part of an ongoing feud between Updike and *Commentary* (on which Updike took a satisfyingly ample revenge in *Bech: A Book*) others have also felt that the charge of 'slickness' or triviality had some substance. While Updike is generally recognised as a consummate stylist, even sympathetic readers have argued that the style conceals a hollow centre. For J. A. Ward, 'the subjects he chooses to write about seem undeserving of his scrupulous care'.[2] Norman Mailer finds his sentences 'precious, overpreened, self-indulgent'. In a swift hatchet-job Joseph Epstein lamented that 'Updike simply cannot pass up an opportunity to tap dance in prose'.[3] Even the Russian poet Yevtushenko told Updike that 'You are a man who could play with giant boulders, but you play with rubber balls'.[4] Some of these accusations should, of course, be discounted as inherently philistine. Style and content are hardly inseparable critical categories and for Updike, language is often a subject in its own right. Particularly in his more self-conscious novels, Updike draws attention to the medium in which he writes, most obviously in the typographic arrangements of *A Month of Sundays* and *Rabbit Redux*, and in the activities of artist-protagonists. Ripostes to the philistines apart, the charge is also answerable on its own terms. Updike has indicated that he undertakes careful research for his novels. *Roger's Version* and *The Coup* provide their own hefty, relevant bibliographies, while the writings of social planners, historians and psychologists inform *The Poorhouse Fair, Couples, The Witches of Eastwick* and the *Rabbit* trilogy. While Updike's major claims, as for any novelist, must rest upon his imaginative and formal achievements, the present study will seek to establish just how far Updike opens up for debate such issues as social engineering, sexual politics, economics and technology. It is also rare to find an author with quite so much to say about work, a topic conspicuously absent from the contemporary American novel. In addition, Updike's interest in the functioning of social groups sets his protagonists off from the tortured individual heroes of so much modern fiction. Even when most alone, the Updike 'hero' is defined in relation to his society, whether a society from which he has been banished (*A Month of Sundays*), an imagined society (*The Coup, The Poorhouse Fair*) or an antagonistic society which threatens his individuality (*Couples*, the *Rabbit* trilogy). For Updike the group *is* often the hero, whether it consists of a coven of witches, ten adulterous couples, the residents of an old-people's home, or the quartet of voices in *Of the Farm*. This social dimension of Updike's fiction has been insufficiently discussed by Updike's critics and deserves further attention.

Those readers who have conceded that Updike has 'something to say' have tended to see the message as deriving from a more prestigious source. Updike has been enthusiastically co-opted into the normative canon of American religio-cultural experience, along with Bellow, Faulkner, Percy and O'Connor. *Rabbit, Run*, in particular, has suffered a plethora of Christian readings, and was even prescribed on one occasion as part of a series of Lenten readings (to the outrage of the congregation).[5] As Updike is a practising Christian, and moreover an intellectually and theologically skilled one, the emphasis is legitimate and has produced some excellent critical studies. However, although religious issues are relevant to any discussion of Updike, it is important to keep them in perspective. John Updike is emphatically not an esoteric writer, nor a rigidly programmed apologist, and it is perfectly possible to understand and appreciate his novels without abstruse theological knowledge. To paraphrase Graham Greene's retort to a similar charge, he is a novelist who happens to be a Christian, rather than a Christian novelist. No one will debate the fact that his fiction refers to Christian beliefs at particular points, nor that some knowledge of Barth, Tillich and Kierkegaard, whose works he has reviewed at length, will deepen our understanding of his intentions. But the realised appeal of the novels is generated by formal achievements, and by the exploration of quite different topics. The social force of religion (as the Protestant ethic, or as the Utopian project, for example) is arguably more important than any overt Christian message. Sexual politics are a focus of more immediate attention than the allocation of sex roles within Christianity, though the latter is relevant. And it is high time that a critic devoted a book-length study to the role of science and technology in Updike's work.

A full discussion, even a listing, of secondary criticism of Updike's works would run to many pages. (Four book-length bibliographies are available). Readers are directed to William Macnaughton's editorial introduction to his collection of critical essays, which surveys current scholarship very thoroughly and with a pleasantly even hand. Book-length studies of Updike include several worth remarking. Alice and Kenneth Hamilton, and George W. Hunt, S.J., have approached the fiction from a religious perspective. The former study, if at times providing overly allegorical readings, usefully explicates the function of Christian allusion. George W. Hunt's volume is altogether more complex and rewarding, particularly in his discussion of Barth, Kierkegaard and Jung, and is easily the best book in this particular context. Three general works (by Rachael Burchard, Charles T. Samuels and Suzanne Uphaus) provide easily accessible introductions, though the best work of this nature is probably Joyce B. Markle's sharply provocative study. Two writers have explored particular themes: pastoralism (Larry Taylor) and ritual (Edward P. Vargo), the former an extremely suggestive treatment which has worn well, the latter somewhat marred by an exaggerated emphasis on myth, ritual and transcendence. More recently, Elizabeth Tallent's ground-breaking exploration of the erotic dimensions of selected works can be recommended. Other recent works includes studies by Donald J. Greiner, Robert Detweiler and George J. Searles (the last-named a comparative and thematic discussion, locally interesting in relation to the *Rabbit* trilogy). Donald Greiner has devoted no less than three books to Updike: to his novels, other work and treatment of adultery. Though Greiner spends far too much time arguing with other critics and surveying their views, his 1981 volume offers the only extended discussion of Updike's poetry, short stories, drama and non-fiction. Robert Detweiler's book, first published in 1972 and comprehensively revised in 1984, is consistently excellent, even within the cramped confines of a series format. Detweiler sets many hares running (some of which will be chased across following pages) and his discussion of the 'non-protagonist strategy' deserves to be singled out. It is worth noting here that although all the above are North American there is no shortage of foreign criticism of Updike. Notable examples include Tony Tanner (Britain), Yves le Pellec[6] (France) and Inna Levidova[7] (USSR) whose perceptive analysis of *The Centaur* as a product of the 1930s creates an image of Updike as a democratic sympathiser with the disinherited which is highly persuasive. Updike's novels have been widely translated abroad, and at home have resulted in a fair degree of fame and fortune, together with literary awards (The National Book Award for *The Centaur*) and election to the National Institute of Arts and Letters (1964) and the American Academy of Arts and Letters (1977). Extensively reviewed, they have also created enough interest to prompt a mass of critical articles in popular and scholarly journals. Within the scope of this study I could not aspire to take issue with, or even to cite, all this secondary work, though I have certainly learned from it all.

What of the man himself? Though critical commonplace enjoins the separation of teller from tale, several salient points emerge from John Updike's biography.[8] Born in 1932, an only child of Dutch, German and Irish descent, Updike was brought up in Shillington, Pennsylvania, where his Lutheran, Democratic family felt the force of the Depression. His grandfather (the model for Hook in *The Poorhouse Fair*) was forced to join a road-repairing crew, his father lost his job as a cable splicer and supported the family thereafter on an annual salary of $1740 as a teacher. For his family, according to Updike, 'work was sacred'. Updike's own interest in work and economics therefore has firm personal bases, as does his prolific output. Updike's mother, herself an aspiring writer, eventually moved the family, which included Updike's grandparents, back to the farm, a model for that in *The Centaur* and *Of the Farm*. Updike's artistic interest was awakened early, by a gift subscription to the *New Yorker* in his eleventh year, though his first ambition was to be a cartoonist. When he entered Harvard in 1950 to study English Literature on a full scholarship, he contributed to the Harvard *Lampoon*. An example of his cartoon work, reproduced in the *Modern Fiction Studies* Updike Special

Number, shows a small boy telling his teacher, 'Miss Gridley, I may have little to say, but I'm determined to say it well'. As recently as 1985 Updike illustrated an autobiographical essay in the *New Yorker* with his own drawings. This interest in the graphic arts, which is particularly relevant to *The Centaur*, *Of the Farm* and *Marry Me*, was developed in 1954 when, together with his first wife Mary, he graduated and spent a year in Oxford at the Ruskin School of Drawing and Fine Art. In the same year he sold his first story to the *New Yorker*, to which he returned to work as a 'Talk of the Town' reporter from 1955–7, during which period he also wrote two (unpublished) novels, *Go Away* and *Home*. Though Updike made a major decision at the age of twenty-five to leave New York and its literary wheeling and dealing, the connection with the *New Yorker* has remained strong. Updike's personal life suggests that he has followed Flaubert's advice, that to be a great writer it is necessary to live like a bourgeois. His working habits are highly ordered. While living in Ipswich, Massachusetts, Updike occupied an office in the centre of town, setting himself a target of three pages per day, the morning occupied with fiction-writing, the afternoon with poetry, reviewing and the 'business' of publishing. (Whole sections of his novels are effectively rewritten at the proof stage.) A practising craftsman who lives by his pen, there is nothing of the campus novelist, media star or ivory-tower writer about Updike. He has cheerfully admitted that he will review almost anything and that, if he had to, he would write the labels for catsup bottles.

A more private motivation for Updike's move to suburban seclusion in Ipswich emerged only recently in a frank autobiographical piece in the *New Yorker* in 1985. Updike suffers from a severe case of psoriasis, a hereditary skin disease (alleviated until recently only by exposure to the sun), in which the skin goes into prolific overproduction and sheds itself. (Updike has used this experience in *The Centaur*). Curiously, Updike owes his draft exemption to it. After Updike's sunless year in England, the examining doctor took one look and classified Updike 4-F. In his own candid admission, Updike, ashamed of his skin, counted himself out of jobs in the public eye, choosing a closeted unseen existence as a writer. Indeed he has even described his early marriage as partly conditioned by the fact that, having found one woman who forgave him his skin, he dared not risk losing her. The move to Ipswich was also motivated by the opportunity provided by its beach for sunbathing, around which Updike's year was structured from Spring to Autumn, with winter back-up trips to the Caribbean, until the development of a new treatment removed the necessity. Updike, however, is not a hermit on the Salinger model, and has travelled in Russia and Eastern Europe (1964–5) as part of a US/USSR cultural exchange, and to Sub-Saharan Africa in 1973, experiences relevant to the *Bech* stories and *The Coup*. In 1973 Ipswich was left behind, together with Updike's first wife from whom he later gained a no-fault divorce, subsequently marrying Martha Bernhard. Updike has frequently been credited with the ability to evoke a palpable sense of place. Others have spoken for Pennyslvania and Massachusetts. Updike's visit to the North of Scotland with Martha, whose ancestors originated there, produced a short story ('Macbech'), set in Caithness, which, for the present writer, amply attests his abilities in this respect.

And so to the present study. In what follows my main intention has been to provide an introduction to Updike's novels which respects both their specificity and their place in Updike's overall development. This study is not organised chronologically. (The *Rabbit* trilogy, appearing at ten-year intervals, makes nonsense of any such arrangement.) Discussions of individual works aim at the illumination of crucial interpretive issues and are oriented towards those works which demand extended treatment. Without engaging in tiresome plot summary, chapters are structured to make each novel's content clear to readers who are unfamiliar with it, and to explain vital background information where necessary. It goes without saying that particular areas of interest (here afforded discrete chapters) overlap into other novels. Readers will readily perceive connections between the aesthetic themes of *Marry Me* and *The Witches of Eastwick*, the Utopian project in *The Poorhouse Fair*, *Couples*, and *The Coup*, and the technological interests of the *Rabbit* trilogy, *The Coup* and *The Witches of Eastwick*, though I have avoided repeating myself reductively upon these topics. Limitations of space have also proscribed a proper treatment of Updike's work in other genres, which must wait for another book. Though the first object has been to provide suggestive interpretations for the student, I also hope that Updike scholars may find food for thought and a few meaty bones for critical contention here. The necessary evils involved in a short introduction to the work of a prolific, contemporary writer are obvious. It must simplify and generalise, mapping out a development which may seem arbitrary, and can offer only interim conclusions. Updike will doubtless continue to surprise his readers.

2

The Social Ethic: *The Poorhouse Fair* and *Couples*

Updike's interest in the functioning of social groups begins with his first novel and extends throughout his fiction. 'Serial characters' (Bech, Rabbit Angstrom, the Maples) whose life-histories are picked up at intervals over several decades, invite a representative or social reading, as they change with their social circumstances. In an associated stratagem in the novel proper, the group is the primary focus, constituting a choral or collective protagonist. Avoiding a personal or *Bildungsroman* plot, Updike uses this collective protagonist to suggest the structures of social change within the structures of narrative. By placing the group at the centre, Updike's fiction thus operates as a critique of narrative practices which select and valorise only major individuals, and focuses attention upon the relationship of individual to society. Two novels are of particular interest in this connection: *The Poorhouse Fair*, in which the different discourses of the inhabitants of a home for the aged are interwoven, and *Couples*, where the experiences of ten suburban pairs interact. Both novels are susceptible to Utopian readings, the one set in a not-too-distant future, the other in the 'post-pill paradise' of the Kennedy–Camelot era, but both are more properly to be understood as dystopian, commenting upon the America in which they were written. In each Updike reflects upon the growing social conformity of the period, in *The Poorhouse Fair* by opposing a non-conformist group to the dictates of the social engineer, in *Couples* by creating a community in which the characters are entirely group-oriented, the products of a corporate ideal.

During the American Fifties the idea that the United States was becoming a slavishly conformist society gained ground among psychologists, social commentators and writers. In a short sketch,

'Anywhere Is Where You Hang Your Hat' (*Assorted Prose*, 6–13),
Updike treated contemporary anonymity in a comic vein, in an
exchange of letters between two residents of Anywhere, USA,
whose average identities derive from a poster illustrating the
correct use of postal zone numbers. *The Poorhouse Fair*, a darker
treatment of social accommodationism, is one of many novels of
the period which interrogate the results of social engineering.
Prominent examples include B. F. Skinner's *Walden Two* (1948),
Ray Bradbury's *Fahrenheit 451* (1953) and Kurt Vonnegut's *Player
Piano* (1954). McCarthyism had revealed the dangers of outbursts
of mass hysteria in response to social repression. In its central
incident *The Poorhouse Fair* recalls Shirley Jackson's treatment of
this theme in 'The Lottery', which, with its account of the stoning
of a scapegoat by a group of average Americans, created a literary
sensation on its *New Yorker* publication in 1948. Written in 1957,
with its events situated some 20 years later, *The Poorhouse Fair*
draws upon a similar vision of a conformist society with a
potentially violent underside. In the novel America is in the
process of 'Settling':

> an increasingly common term that covered the international
> stalemate, the general economic equality, the population
> shifts to the 'vacuum states', and the well-publicized physical
> theory of entropia, the tendency of the universe toward
> eventual homogeneity. . . . This end was inevitable, no new
> cause for heterogeneity being, without supernaturalism,
> conceivable. (65/60)[9]

With its domestic problems resolved by scientific humanism,
poverty eradicated and racial prejudice eliminated, America
under President Lowenstein represents a secular Utopia, in
peaceful coexistence with the 'London Pacts' and the 'Eurasian
Soviet'.

As an apostle of this process, Conner, the director of the
Diamond County Poorhouse, is intent upon forcing its inmates to
cohere into a homogenous group. For the inmates, however,
nothing is settled. Political conflicts, philosophical and religious
problems are continually debated afresh. To Conner, these are
dead issues; he completely misses the relevance of one such debate
(on the Civil War and slavery, 92/82) to the residents' own
situation. Where Conner's mock-anthropological terminology

dehumanises the inmates, who appear from his distant bureaucratic citadel as 'an ant colony' (50/47), the old people enjoy a variety of carefully differentiated voices and visions. Where Conner looks forward to a secular, homogeneous paradise for all, the inmates, in one of their many discussions, envisage a whole array of vividly imagined and contrasting heavens.

Although supernaturalism contributes heterogeneity to this small social group, Updike speedily undercuts any easy nostalgia for that older Protestant America which they represent. In the initial scene of the novel the old men discover labels screwed to their chairs. Though Conner's demogogic desire to see the inmates duly placed and docketed makes him Updike's prime satiric target, the sense in which the older generation's respect for authority derives from a preceding creed is also underlined. When anarchic Gregg occupies Hook's chair Hook merely adopts his usual position to Gregg's left, displacing Lucas one chair further along the row. In a comically Beckettian scene of musical chairs, the minimal rebellion collapses as the men shuffle back into line, submitting to Hook's authority. Hook's clinching argument for the desirability of knowing one's place associates Conner's regimentation and bureaucratic supervision with an image of moral book-keeping consonant with the Protestant ethic: the men's proximity to 'the Line' (death) means that they have their 'accounts watched very close' (5/10). The ambivalent relation of the inmates to freedom is also focused in the fates of two animals. The one, a feral cat, free but hideously mangled in an accident, is entrapped and put out of its misery at Conner's behest. Though Conner proceeds from the best of motives, the gloating pleasure of his henchman Buddy strongly suggests the truth of Thoreau's remark that, if you see a man approach you with the obvious intention of doing you good, you should run for your life. The other creature, a glossy parakeet, reveals the advantages of snug confinement as opposed to dangerous freedom. Though a being, like the inmates, with no apparent 'reason' or 'function' (Conner's watchwords), the escaped bird provides a glorious vision of splendour admist the sensual deprivation of the bedridden, much as the inmates' lack of occupation frees them for a potentially rich speculative existence. It is an inmate, anxious for its safety, who restores the bird to its cage.

In the action of the novel three further events interrupt the status quo: the accidental destruction of the poorhouse wall, the stoning, and the fair itself, each of which dramatises symbolically a different image of society. In the first incident a truck-driver, taunted by Gregg as a conformist 'company man' (59/55), breaches the enclosing poorhouse wall. Significantly the old wall, an apparently solid and well-crafted structure, reveals in its collapse a hollow centre, filled with rubble. The resultant debris provides the ammunition for the stoning of Conner, who discovers that he has succeeded in engineering a cohesive group only at his own expense. Conner's abolition of an older, if hollow and rotten, social structure, in the service of a corporate ideal, has transformed the inmates from a small, richly differentiated society into a mob acting with one violent will. At the fair where the inmates sell their own handicrafts, the societies of past and present confront each other. Throughout the novel a pervasive metaphor has associated Amy Mortis's handmade quilts with a social fabric which combines variety with design. Both Hook and Conner employ this metaphor. Hook, reviewing his past, seeks in that 'full bolt of cloth' (37/37), the 'deeper dyed thread' (27/29) which will reveal the significant pattern of his existence. Conner himself ascribes to the belief that 'it strengthens . . . a communal fabric to have running through it strands of private ownership' (19/23). Neither man, however, enjoys the total vision of Amy Mortis. To take a single guiding idea (individualism or collectivism) and attempt to follow that thread through all of life's occasions, is to miss the significance of the thread itself, whose function is to add to the complexity and interest of life's total pattern.[10] A single quilt of Amy's contains within it a whole series of different worlds, its squares featuring rivers, hills, a temple, a plaid cross, children, the alphabet, even a patch of savage red. The image of the quilt suggests the need for a form of social organisation woven of numerous threads and patterns, in which the individual nature of the different patches can be respected. These are, however, the last quilts Amy will make (171/152). In the new homogeneous America, figured cloth is unobtainable, plainness prevails. The quilts are none the less highly attractive to the townspeople, for whom they fulfil 'a keen subversive need' (145/126). How that need will be met in the future remains questionable. At the end of the novel the old people's voices are crowded out by the anonymous utterances of the townspeople, presented merely as a montage of scraps of dialogue. Though unpatterned, these apparently random fragments are uniformly concerned with purely physical needs (sex, health and pleasure). The omniscient narrator comments regretfully that 'Heart had gone out of these people; health was the principal thing' (158/137), but goes on to assume Conner's anthropological tone:

> Highly neural, brachycephalic, uniquely able to oppose their thumbs to the four other digits, they bred within elegant settlements, and both burned and interred their dead. (158/137)

In the background the old-fashioned military marches played by the band underline the extent to which 'the conception "America" had died in their skulls' (159/138). Though the music is described as colouring the air with the colours of the flag, 'the weave of the orchestration was tattered and torn' (123/108). While Updike acknowledges that America can no longer be sustained by its previous creeds, no new synthesis emerges from their collapse. Updike himself described *The Poorhouse Fair* as saying No 'to social homogenization' (*Picked-Up Pieces*, p. 503) but the novel remains diagnostic rather than prescriptive.

In *Couples*, a novel which also features a collective protagonist, Updike turned his attention to the various remedies on offer. In the Fifties several neo-Freudian thinkers proposed differing diagnoses and prescriptions for the malaise in American society, in terms which centre upon notions of freedom and repression.[11] Herbert Marcuse (*Eros and Civilisation*, 1955) argued for a new polymorphous sexuality to replace the repressions on which American society appeared to be founded. Rather similarly, Norman O. Brown (*Life Against Death*, 1959) supported the need for an erotic society in which conscious play would be substituted for alienated labour. In contrast, in *The Sane Society* (1956), Erich Fromm described life in twentieth-century democracy as marked by a deep-seated craving to escape the freedom recently gained from clerical and secular authorities. In his account, rather than pursuing individual goals, the human being flees into the industrial machine, gaining a sense of self only from conformity to the majority. Instead of perceiving himself as the active bearer of his own potential, such an individual sees himself as a commodity or investment, an impoverished or alienated 'thing' dependent on external powers. In his description of Park Forest, Illinois, a suburban development, Fromm analyses its inhabitants as seeking identity in social conformity rather than in individualism. Indiscriminate sociability, 'outgoing' behaviour, lack of privacy, and the relentless 'talking out' of each others' problems in ersatz psychologese characterise this social group which engulfs new arrivals. One inhabitant's comment on the need for group participation is suggestive:

> I've brought out two couples myself. . . . Whenever we see someone who is shy and withdrawn we make a special effort with them. (Fromm, p. 157)

Fromm's source for his analysis of suburban life, William H. Whyte, provides a fuller description of the suburb which has interesting points of contact with *Couples*. Like Fromm, Marcuse and Brown, Whyte perceived the decline of the Protestant ethic as of prime significance. For Whyte, twentieth-century America is characterised by the emergence of the 'organisation man', the individual who belongs to the organisation, whether within a large corporation, as researcher in a government laboratory, doctor in a corporate clinic or member of a church hierarchy. In his view, while officially holding to the Protestant ethic (individualism, thrift, work, competition), Americans are in fact increasingly organised collectively. The organisation man's need for a body of thought which will morally legitimise the pressures of society upon the individual, validating his activity, much as the Protestant ethic used to do, produces the 'social ethic', a slowly coalescing creed in which three beliefs are fundamental: that the group is the source of creativity, that 'belongingness' is the ultimate need of the individual, and that such belongingness may be achieved by the application of science. In this ethic man is of himself isolated and meaningless, becoming worthwhile only as he collaborates with others. By applying techniques which have worked in the physical sciences to human relations, an exact science of man can be evolved, as in personality measurement, behaviourism, group dynamics and social engineering of various types. Obstacles to social consensus may thus be eliminated, creating an equilibrium in which the needs of society and of the individual are one and the same. The goal is therefore Utopian, aimed at a future, finite, achievable harmony. It is also hedonistic. Whyte quotes one motivation researcher's statement that one of the basic problems of American prosperity is to give people the justification to enjoy it, to demonstrate that the hedonistic approach to life is a moral one. Social controls thus operate covertly. New magic terms are created, which combine manipulation with moral sanction (group therapist, integrative leader, social diagnostician). In the broad social sphere increased deference to the group produces a preoccupation with team work (conference, workshop, seminar, project team, think tank). In the personal creed of belongingness, problems can be 'talked out', adjustment is the goal, and the tensions of independence are regarded as a sickness. The idea that conflicting allegiances may safeguard the individual as well as abrade him is sloughed over. For Whyte this vain quest for a Utopian equilibrium, the soft-minded denial that there is conflict between individual and society, and the spurious peace of mind offered, constitute the major flaws in the social ethic. As he points out, it is possible to believe that man has a social obligation, without believing that group harmony is the test of it. In the social ethic, however, man's obligation is not to the community in the broad sense, but to the actual physical one about him. People cooperate just to cooperate, rather than for substantive reasons or goals.

Whyte's bulky volume, *The Organization Man* (1956), follows the typical product of these beliefs from college through indoctrination in corporate life to the new suburbs, which offer a preview of the future direction of the social ethic. For Whyte, suburbia is the ultimate expression of the interchangeability sought by large corporations. It is politically conservative, classless, at least in intention, and levels out human differences. Democrats tend to become Republicans in the suburbs, and religious affiliations are watered down. (Fundamentalists are likely to become Methodists or Presbyterians.) Typically such communities include a large proportion of college graduates, mobile at the behest of their organisations. Park Forest was swiftly settled by research chemists, airline pilots, the military, and executives, mostly aged between 25 and 35 and married. Newcomers are swiftly educated by the group in taste, clothes and behaviour. Inconspicuous consumption (keeping down with the Joneses) is the norm, in order to avoid flouting the sensibilities of others, and to conform with the egalitarian ideal. Whyte went on to analyse the basic mechanics of suburban social life, examining the different groups of couples which tended to party together. Friendship here was based on propinquity, the geographical layout of the suburb tending to encourage the formation of certain sets. The size of such groups rarely swells beyond twelve couples, largely because the size of suburban living-rooms prevents larger gatherings. On the credit side the group diminishes loneliness, the couples forming a mutual assistance pact, replacing for each other the absent extended family of previous years. Neighbourliness fills a social void and participation in a variety of civic activities becomes an end in itself. On the debit side the group can be a tyrant as well as a friend, tough on anyone who does not fit in and capable of punishing the deviant cruelly. While Whyte focuses on a package suburb, he applies his insights equally to small towns colonised by organisation men. Whyte's suburban denizens differ from Updike's in only one vital respect. In the package suburb adultery seemed to be unusual, since the spatial organisation of the development, and its picture-window architecture, made philandering all too visible. Presumably this is why Updike chose a small town, rather than a collection of 'little boxes', though as we shall see, the organisation of domestic space is of major importance in Tarbox too.

In number, as well as in other respects, the ten couples of the Tarbox group exemplify the traits outlined by Whyte. Apart from the Guerins and Thornes, all are recent arrivals: the Applebys and Smiths in the mid-fifties, the Ongs and Saltzes in 1957, the Hanemas and Gallaghers in 1958, the Constantines in 1960 and the Whitmans in the present (1963). Most of the men are college graduates, all but the Guerins have children, and their ranks encompass Jews, Catholics and members of various Protestant denominations. Apart from the Whitmans they seem to be Republicans, though their involvement in political and religious matters is fairly minimal. Their origins are diverse, including Korean John Ong, Midwest-Dutch Piet, Southern Foxy, Georgene from Philadelphia, Janet from Buffalo, Japanese-Portuguese Bernadette and Irish Matt Gallagher. A high proportion of the males are connected by their occupations with science and large corporations. Ben Saltz miniaturises components for the space programme, and is employed, like research physicist John Ong, by the government. Eddie Constantine, a pilot, is also in government aeronautics. Ken Whitman works as a biochemist in a university. Both Frank and Harold are in 'securities', in a bank and a brokerage firm respectively. Piet and Matt, working for their own firm, are apparent exceptions, but as the builders of tacky new ranch-houses they service suburban needs. Though largely middle-class, inconspicuous consumption is the group norm, exemplified by Bea Guerin, cooking her own lamb, despite the fact that her husband is rich enough not to work.

Importantly, in its early stages the group is founded on innocently Utopian principles. The Applebys and Smiths are described as rebelling against the constricting habits of their wealthy upbringing, determined to rear their families without 'help', doing their own housework and home repairs, driving secondhand cars and using the public school system. In a social climate which, in the Fifties, is still 'furtively hedonist' (106/120), the couples have moved beyond the stratified society of their past, settling in Tarbox in order to improvise a simpler way of life, specifically designed to replace the Protestant ethic.

> Duty and work yielded as ideals to truth and fun. Virtue was no longer sought in temple or market place but in the home – one's own home and then the homes of one's friends.   (106/121)

Slowly, however, the original liberated Utopia yields to an erotically structured group and thence to final conformity as suburbia takes over. On arrival in Tarbox, Janet Appleby rejects the indigenous party-giving group, repelled by their heavy drinking, bridge parties and infidelities. At the end of the novel the wheel turns full circle as the newest arrival, Deb Reinhardt, rejects the couples' 'crummy crowd', in order to form her own set, the liberal, asexual 'Shakers'. The surviving couples take to bridge; the Saltzes and the new Hanemas move on. In the intervening period, Updike charts the ecology of the group and its slow evolution from Protestant ethic to Utopian ideals and thence to accommodation to the social norm. Like Whyte's suburbanites, the couples are relentlessly gregarious, structuring their year around a succession of seasonal games, discussing their most intimate problems in frank detail and analysing each other's adjustment in psychological terms. For all their code of belongingness, however, when a group member deviates from the norm, the couples mobilise to punish the deviant, either by indirect attack (a series of party games which target a victim) or in the case of adulterers, by social exclusion. Ironic light is therefore cast on their secular humanist creed, summarised by Freddy

Thorne, its main mouthpiece: 'We're all put here to humanize each other' (148/168). According to Angela, Freddy sees the couples as 'a magic circle of heads to keep the night out. He told me he gets frightened if he doesn't see us over a weekend. He thinks we've made a church of each other' (7/14). As other critics have pointed out, a profusion of Edenic and Biblical imagery reinforces the impression of the group as having founded a substitute secular religion.

Although Updike's interest in religious matters is not at issue, it is important to note that the structure of the novel calls attention to its social theme. Most of the details of the group's formation are not provided until the second chapter (Applesmiths and Other Games) which predates the opening sequence. This disruption of chronology has two major effects, bearing upon form and theme. First the reader enters the novel *in medias res*, encountering the couples at an opening party. Much as any new arrival in Tarbox, we have to make sense of a diffuse group, identifying its members and its internal dynamics only tentatively. Though newcomer Foxy Whitman is the reader's surrogate, she is equally confused by the group. Updike therefore constructs an implied reader as suburban newcomer, picking out features of group-membership and norms, without the benefit of a formal introduction from the omniscient narrator. The novel thus sidesteps overt 'social diagnosis', inviting the reader first to respond personally to a group, rather than to an established narrative authority. A variety of narrative features (stream of consciousness, internal monologue, interpolated letters, action through dialogue, word games) all combine to present the reader with a series of different discourses, in which no one voice is dominant. When the postponed background detail is presented in the second section, which provides the characters with their life-histories, the reader feels both relief as confusions are cleared up, and a simultaneous check on his own imaginative freedom. The manner of narration therefore situates the individual reader between conflicting social norms (group ethic, authoritarian control) abrading the authority of narrative, undercutting any one individualist focus, and maintaining the reader in creative tension.

In addition the flashback second chapter has important thematic implications. If the novel is not a sociological report, it also avoids becoming a theological treatise. The chapter, concerned only with the Applebys and Smiths, largely excludes religious symbolism, setting the group's activities in relation to a longer period of social change. The Applebys and Smiths undergo a representative evolution in which the corporate ideal conditions their private lives. Although domestic adultery is the major topic, the language of the husbands' trades permeates their erotic activities. Initially the couples are brought together by the slump in the money market in 1962. Frank invites Marcia to sexualise their friendship because 'with this sloppy market running, it's probably the best investment left' (112/128). Harold is initially uneasy about betraying Marcia with Janet, whom he sees as a 'bad investor' (119/135). At first he is content to benefit instead from Marcia's newfound erotic versatility: 'Brokers reaped in fair and foul weather' (131/149). His meetings with Janet, engineered ostensibly to talk out their problem, entrance him none the less with their insights into the group, which he now sees 'through a whole new set of windows' (125/142). As a result, Harold's house, a modern construction with walls of sliding plate glass, becomes 'more transparent; its privacy had been surrendered' (121/138). When Janet finally procures proof of Marcia's adultery and propositions Harold on a pile of dirty laundry, the pair go no further, embarrassed by their proximity to the picture window. As the imagery punningly suggests, however, they eventually wash their dirty linen in public. Moreover, when the men formally swap wives (without consulting the ladies) they are corporately motivated. Frank, the more powerful businessman, has given Harold commissions as a broker. Harold, indebted, yields:

> There is always a time to sell; the trick of the market is to know when. Janet waited like a stack of certain profit.   (150/170)

If the wife-swapping itself foregrounds the norm of interchangeability, with the wives as exchangeable commodities, later events confirm the suggestion that the two couples have slipped from Utopian ideals to group behaviour. Janet is reduced to a topic of conversation as the others 'discuss her "problem" with her as if it might lie anywhere but with them' (161/182), and eventually despatch her to a psychiatrist, brushing aside her own sense of corruption. 'What they took to be morality proved to be merely consciousness of the other couples watching them' (158/179). The picture-window world of suburbia, with its social ethic and corporate ideals, has triumphed.

In like fashion the occupations of the other males permeate their personal lives, at times comically, at others ironically. Freddy, the dentist, is obsessed with death and decay. Ken Whitman, intent on researching the chemical bonds which hold life together, loses any real contact with his wife and new baby. Piet Hanema's occupation as a builder is of more general symbolic significance. In Tarbox the way in which the couples organise their domestic space is an index to the state of their marriages, from the square restricted Saltzes' narrow house, to the home of the moneyed Guerins, expensively restored yet remaining 'a touch off true' (81/94). In the novel, Updike makes social concepts immediately graspable through architectural metaphors, particularly in terms of the opposition of old and new ethics. The first chapter, Welcome to Tarbox, establishes Piet as caught between old and new creeds, fearing freedom, yet ambivalent towards the security offered by the emergent domestic ethic. While his first love is renovation, involving the application of careful craftsmanship to the seventeenth-century Puritan dwellings in the town, visible remains of the Protestant ethic, he is increasingly forced to construct suburban developments for cash, specifically the ranch-houses on Indian Hill, based on canned blueprints from an architectural factory in Chicago, and constructed from mass-produced components. Piet's own home a graceful eighteenth-century farmhouse, low-ceilinged, encircled by woods and a protective high hedge, expresses his delight in security. 'All houses, all things that enclosed, pleased Piet' (5/11). In contrast, Angela had wanted a property with an Atlantic view, the flimsy, jerry-built Robinson place, later acquired by the shaky Whitman menage. When the novel opens, insomniac Piet is discovered, uneasily musing on death, and seeking comfort in the snug angles of his house, with its foil-lined attic and freshly cemented basement. He is, however, equally reassured by the regular revolutions of his daughter's caged hamster, a more disquieting image of his own attraction to secure structures.

Piet's renovatory skills are the topic of conversation at the Guerins' party, where the enclosed, self-restricting nature of Tarbox society is ironically demonstrated. Conversation turns to Gertrude Tarbox, an old lady whose walls are so stacked with issues of *National Geographic* that Frank jokes that with the arrival of the November 1984 issue she will be crushed to death (a somewhat pat opposition of vast outer vistas and narrowing inner spaces). The talk moves on to the recent Thresher disaster in which members of a submarine crew were crushed, and to a Poe story in which walls squeeze in upon the characters. When Ken jokes that the author of the tale is 'I. M. Flat, a survivor in two dimensions' (30/38), his subsequent description of his job, thinly slicing starfish, prompts Janet's flirtatious, 'And then do they survive, in two dimensions?' (33/41). The conversation culminates in an exchange between Freddy and Foxy, centred upon Piet. For Freddy Piet is neurotic, over-obsessed with work and the church. When Foxy asks him to define 'neurotic' he counters:

> 'You haven't told me that what you mean by character.'
> 'Perhaps', Foxy said, scornfully bright, 'we mean the same thing'. (36/44)

Quite overtly the scene suggests the possible effects of an enclosing security upon the free individual. For Foxy personal eccentricity is character, for Freddy a neurotic failure of adjustment. For the reader, encountering the group for the first time at this point, the participants are not yet fully three-dimensional; their outlines have yet to be rounded out. In the novel the relative 'flatness' of many characters, adversely commented upon by critics, serves to highlight their relation to an inward-looking conformist society. The literary question is also the social: Will these people develop into characters, or will they simply survive in two dimensions?

Piet's relationship with Georgene at first seems to suggest that he will be drawn from the enclosed secure world towards a freer, if more dangerous existence. At the Applebys' party Piet, frustrated by the enclosure of the crowded playroom, its windows painted shut, feels that 'it's getting too suburban in here' (12/19). With Georgene he has the sensation of 'a going from indoors to outdoors' (224/250). Their affair none the less founders upon the opposition between the Protestant ethic and the new Utopianism. In the scene in which the couple make love on Georgene's sunroof, pre-lapsarian imagery predominates. 'Guileless' Georgene, unashamedly naked, welcomes Piet to the 'post-pill paradise'. Piet, however, fears that they will 'embarrass God' (54/64). He is equally unsuccessful in suppressing thoughts of work, his mind moving comically to 'Ruberoid Rolled Roofing, mineralized, $4.25 a roll in 1960. He had laid this deck' (52/62). Importantly Piet snatches his meetings with Georgene during working hours.

Although ostensibly operating on the work ethic he has actually used his work as a cover for his hedonistic activities, much as he later uses attendance at church to meet Foxy. When he transfers his attentions to Foxy, he speedily reverts to his original creed. One scene makes this point explicitly. In order to conceal the nature of Georgene's telephone appeal from his listening partner, Piet couches his responses in terms of his trade. When Georgene asks why he has not called he tells her that 'the orders are slow coming through this time of year' (217/243). When she begs him to visit her he answers that 'the estimate looks discouraging'. Georgene's account of her husband's phallic deficiencies (he wilts) prompts Piet's 'we're speaking of upright supports'. He rejects her plea for 15 minutes ('we're behind schedule now') and as she breaks down in tears, rings off cruelly with 'Watch out for seepage'. The conversation reveals Piet's real attitude to Georgene, reduced here, in the deceptive fiction of a business caller, from free erotic individual to a job of work, a thing. Piet's first covert essay into an erotic Utopianism ends with a pragmatic retreat into the security of an older ethic.

Piet's church-going strikes a similarly ironic note of self-deception and of security and freedom entangled. On the one hand Piet recognises the Congregational church as a poor substitute for his original sterner Dutch-Reformed faith. He winces at the abolitionist hymn in which the congregation pose as slaves, and is repelled by the minister's equally slavish sermon, designed for businessmen, with its emphasis on security and the corporate ideal:

> The man Jesus does not ask us to play a long shot. . . . No, he offers us present security, four-and-a-half per cent compounded every quarter. (21/28)

The architecture of the church, however, a much-restored Greek temple, with alabaster effects skilfully mimicked in wood, attracts him, its well-joined wood apparently denying decay and death, and providing a safe refuge. Prayer offers a similar satisfaction. When it works Piet seems to himself to be 'in the farthest corner of a deep burrow, a small endearing hairy animal, curled up as if to hibernate' (18/25). As the image suggests, Piet's allegiance is to the church as sheltering structure, rather than to a body of challenging religious beliefs.

The opposition between security and dangerous freedom is further developed in the plot in the death of Nancy's hamster, an event which occurs at the close of the first section. Piet notes, without applying the comment to himself, that Nancy had been unable to believe 'that any creature might have wits too dim to resent such captivity' (76/89). She therefore enlarged the hamster's cage with a flimsy construction of window screens. Exploring, the hamster escapes into a 'sudden heaven' (76/89) of new sensual experiences, but his 'adventure' is terminated by a neighbouring cat. On one level the episode has a predictive quality. Adultery is subsequently described as 'a way of giving yourself adventures. Of getting out in the world and seeking knowledge' (343/380). With knowledge, however, comes death. Georgene took Piet outdoors into paradise; he retreats into a safer shelter. Foxy will bring more dangerous knowledge. At this point in the novel the episode also serves to demonstrate the complacency of Piet and Angela. Angela simply sidesteps the fact of death. A new interchangeable hamster will be purchased. Piet responds by constructing a more secure cage, built to his own design from odds and ends of lumber, suggesting a parallel with his own set of beliefs, assembled in similarly haphazard and pragmatic fashion to promote security. Ironically, although the cage is enlarged to form a child-size shelter, Nancy dislikes it, imagining that it is a 'little prison' (94/108) destined for her. Both parents, in their attempt to avoid confronting an uncomfortable event, combine to enclose and diminish Nancy's world. The point is generalised in Piet's two subsequent visits to his workers. At Indian Hill he discovers that the ranch-houses are probably being constructed on the site of an Indian burial ground, but is cheered by the lack of concern shown by the men who casually push exhumed bones back beneath the surface. The second visit, to a garage which is being constructed on old-fashioned artisanal principles, ends with Piet cutting the job short for financial reasons, compromising his own ethic. As this first movement of the novel demonstrates, Piet's flirtation with freedom ends in a renewed assertion of his need for security. Erotic Utopianism of the type advocated by Marcuse and Brown has been tested and found wanting, and with his Protestant ethic already attenuated, Piet has begun to compromise with the social ethic.

The nature of this compromise is brought out in Piet's relationship with Foxy. Ostensibly Foxy also yearns for open spaces and freedom. In the initial sequence of the third section, Thin Ice, she demands open shelving. Piet's argument for 'spaces you can close' (186/209) falls on deaf ears: 'I want open shelves and open doorways and everything open to the sea and the sea air' (187/209). As Piet reconstructs her home, tearing down a servants' wing and removing boards from windows, light floods the house. Though the job is a commercial loser, Piet enjoys the traditional procedures involved, and it appears that he has renegotiated the terms of his existence, to combine traditional secure structures with a degree of freedom. To Piet Foxy becomes 'an entire house . . . its structure incandescent' (204/228), whereas Angela, in contrast, now appears as a 'boarded door' (204/228). When she describes Piet as a caged animal, he accuses her: 'But Angel, who made the cage' (205/230). Surfacing from a vexed night with Angela, Piet now registers his home as confining, noting its narrow stairs, cramped hall and living-room darkened by lilacs. While apparently providing a freer space, however, Foxy does so in terms which speedily domesticate their relationship. Her first overture is couched in reassuring terms: 'Aren't we in our house? Aren't you building this house for me?' (201/225). Word play and imagery suggest a qualifying irony directed at their apparent freedom. Piet finds Foxy alone because the workmen have left to look for 'a male threader and a coupling' (197/221). The physical details of their love-making emphasise Piet as builder. Foxy's body has a wooden texture, which he turns 'on the lathe of the light' (202/226), and her pregnancy forces 'homely accommodations upon them' (202/226). In her tent-shaped maternity smock she projects an image of a shelter which is lighter, and yet which clearly satisfies Piet's deep-seated Oedipal desire for security. Foxy appeals in terms which carefully cater both to Piet's emergent social ethic and to his residual Calvinism. Piet had described America as 'an unloved child smothered in candy' (200/224). Foxy, a sterner mother figure, seduces him over sour lemon squash. So successful is her deception that later, looking back on the affair, Piet is to miss 'the thrift of a double life, the defiant conservation' (284/315). Adultery is sanctioned as a form of thrift, filling his hours much as carpentry does.

Just how unliberated this particular adultery is, is revealed in a series of word games. In the first, Impressions, group members are ascribed a social or political identity by the rest of the group, which they then have to discover for themselves. To the informed reader the group are unsurprisingly affectionate in their impressions of Piet as Ho Chi Minh, 'the enemy of our democracy' (176/198), who is described as grey, conformist and ordinary, 'an idol with its head knocked off' (173/195) in a pacified landscape. The game vividly suggests the group's desire to assimilate Piet to conformity with the social ethic. More generally, the focus on social or political personalities implies a coercive society, pulling the strings and directing its members into conditioned roles, which are essentially dangerous to the preservation of a living democracy. In addition, although Piet's fictional identity is given in advance, Foxy's has to be guessed. Though the clues lead to an identification with 'whorish' Christine Keeler, the guess is not confirmed at the end of the game, so that as readers we have to guess along with Foxy. While the probable solution expresses the group's hostility to Foxy and undermines any Utopian image of her eroticism, the reader shares her bewildered position. The construction of the scene thus provides the reader first with security (we are in the know, part of the group) and then with uncertainty, mystification and doubt (we are aligned with the victim of the group). Importantly the game is also our first clue to Piet and Foxy's adultery, preceding actual description, so that we are guessing on several levels. Their affair is therefore discovered to us through the medium of socially ascribed roles, neither of which suggest freedom of choice.

A second word game occurs at the Constantines' party. Already tensions are surfacing among the couples and the group is beginning to splinter. Although the house is large, much of its space is consumed by stairways, halls and closets so that the party splits into several rooms. Two conversations run in tandem here. In one, Irene and Frank are arguing about the Massachusetts Fair Housing Bill. The bill, designed to promote racial integration of neighbourhoods, draws attention to the issue of social engineering through the organisation of domestic space. Ben's drunken remarks rephrase the debate in aesthetic terms:

> What should the aesthetics of modern housing be? Should there be any beyond utility and cost? . . . . perhaps a more oral and sacramental culture has an instinctive sense of beauty that capitalism with its assembly-line method of operation destroys. (235/262)

The aesthetic effects of the couples' own activities are indicated in the foreground conversation, as they read Freddy's playlet. Punningly erotic, the names of Freddy's characters (Eric Shun, Ora Fiss, Cunny Lingus) are the ultimate in flatness, as is the play, in which sexual entry is to be followed onstage by the appearance of Auntie Climax. Terry's comment may be taken to apply equally to play and novel: 'It's not even begun. It's a cast of characters' (230/257). The couples decide that 'we need more plot' (231/258), and develop the play through their own fantasies. Where Impressions connected the characters with the political effects of the social ethic, the word games at the Constantines' demonstrate just how impoverished their inner imaginations are. (In the background, Carol's mediocre, muddled paintings confirm the point.) Asked to name the most wonderful thing in the world, the characters make tell-tale responses. The first three choices are domestic, a baby's fingernails (Carol) a sleeping woman (Piet) and the music Bach wrote to support his seventeen children (Terry), while Foxy's choice, the Eucharist, may well be a blasphemous reference to her oral erotic activities with Piet. Angela selects the stars, not as an image of infinite space, but on the grounds that they are fixed and unchanging entities, which dwarf the human being. The game ends in argument over Freddy's choice, the human capacity for self-deception. Piet's comment sums up the major flaw in the group's Eden:

> What impresses me isn't so much human self-deception as human ingenuity in creating unhappiness. We believe in it. Unhappiness is us. From Eden on we've voted for it. (242/270)

The entire scene suggests that conformity, the attenuated individual, and lack of creativity are the results of social engineering. Bland happiness is not enough. People need tensions as the erotic play needs more plot. In their passive Utopianism, their belief in a tension-free static harmony attainable on earth, the characters are diminishing to new levels of flatness.

Ben Saltz's fate amplifies this reading. Sacked from his job for his adultery-inspired absences, Ben has freedom thrust upon him, and is promptly excluded by the other couples. Ironically his allegiance to the group creed has compromised the work ethic. Unemployed, Ben reverts to orthodox religion. Though Piet dreads meeting him, when he catches sight of him it is 'a glimpse, shockingly, of happiness' (255/284). Leaving work and group ethics behind him Ben has 'touched bottom and found himself at rest, safe' (255/284). Piet, however, is still caught in the contradictions of the two creeds. His latest project, the enlargement of a local restaurant in fraudulently antiqued style, is entirely appropriate to his position. Researching the details of colonial carpentry, he is demoralized by the attempt to turn these 'ethical old specifications' (267/297) into modern quaintness. The gulf between old and new creeds is now unbridgeable, and Piet's easy synthesis is exposed. Because the new project is a rush job, he is also unable to meet Foxy and is left with unresponsive Angela, the latter, as the chapter ends, engrossed in the latest Salinger novel, ironically entitled *Raise High the Roof Beam, Carpenters*. Foxy's letters, re-read at this point, emphasise Piet's lack of freedom. In one letter she asks: 'Isn't it our utter captivity that makes us, in our few stolen afternoons together, so free?' (263/292). The date of the letter, the Fourth of July, implicitly suggests a connection with wider issues of political freedom, a connection made explicit in subsequent events.

In the final movement of the novel, three deaths (Kennedy, Foxy's embryonic child, John Ong) reveal the impossibility of the couples' ideals of unchanging harmony and the high price of their beliefs. Politically, violent change occurs, while the party on the day of Kennedy's death draws Piet and Foxy back together with personal consequences. John Ong, a refugee from political horrors, finds death as well as secure asylum in America. Throughout the novel the couples have steadily excluded external political events. As Piet comments, 'News happened to other people' (214/240). Kennedy's death confirms their solipsistic isolation. After the first announcement of the assassination the radio resumes its bland music, just as the couples resume their usual activities. The Thornes refuse to cancel their planned party, at which the friends simply reconstruct their own illusive group, retreating from the implications of a major political event to celebrate their own belongingness. Piet, at first, resists the idea of dancing on Kennedy's grave, but Angela insists: 'We can't let Roger and Carol do it alone. They're getting too embarrassed' (306/339). Loyalty to the immediate physical group triumphs over any broader social obligation. The background music at the party suggests both a diminished secular world, and a collective illusion. The songs, 'Stars fell on Alabama', 'Soft as the Starlight', 'It Must Have Been Moonglow', 'Wrap Your Troubles in Dreams', form a succession which moves from the idea of a fallen star (Kennedy as a fallen idol) to an immersion in dream. The quoted line 'Close your eyes' underlines the couples' wilful blindness to the political, while the following 'Castles may tumble, that's fate after all' crystallises their easy acceptance of events, as if fate swayed their existence. Indeed the sense of a shrinking universe is actually matter for celebration among them. Matt comments happily that the shortage of space downtown is good news for builders. Harold demythologies Kennedy as 'a cleverly manufactured politician' (310/343) whose death will be good for business. Later, Foxy psychologises the event, describing Kennedy as a victim of Marina Oswald's sexual rejection of her husband (449/496). When Oswald is shot, on television, Ruth's question, 'Was that real?' (319/354), says it all.

In plot terms Kennedy's death brings Piet and Foxy back together. All Fall Piet has felt a growing insecurity: 'My whole life seems just a long falling' (312/345). At the party he turns to Foxy for reassurance, as his grotesque desire to breastfeed indicates. Trapped in the bathroom by Angela, however, his only recourse is to free-fall from the window. Foxy's comment that the leap was unnecessary, 'You were clearly in love with the idea of jumping' (316/350), suggests Piet's growing desire to escape from both the domestic trap and the paradisal illusion. In the background Bea points out a shooting star, while Angela, described as suspended above them, floats and shimmers downstairs. The implications of fallen angels, falling stars and a diminished democracy are carefully interwoven through the stellar imagery, which suggests the falsity of a secular paradise, the inevitability of fall, and the attenuated freedom of the group. A further adultery, between Piet and Bea, underlines the dealthy stasis of an erotic Utopia, and establishes the connection between passivity and cruelty. Piet, 'having exploited her passivity in all positions' (336/371), slaps Bea hard. Their orgasm is described as a 'crisisless osmosis' (336/372), as if they were no longer individuals but merely cells conjoining. Cruelty is the product of the lack of tension in their relationship, which is not so much life-affirming as deathly and sterile.

The murderous consequences of the couples' passivity are dramatised in the abortion of Foxy's child. Like Piet, Freddy is

able to use his work for non-ethical purposes and consents to find
an abortionist, in exchange for a night with Angela. The
particular situation – sex in exchange for death – mimics the
underlying logic of the couples' creed. Angela, newly converted to
adjustment, prefaces her night of love with Freddy with a
discussion of Freud's concept of the death-instinct: 'He says we,
all animals, carry our deaths in us – that the organic wants to be
returned to the inorganic state' (367/406). While the
juxtaposition of this comment with an abortion is particularly
horrifying, her comments are also borne out in erotic terms.
Freddy, as passive as Bea, remains all too inorganic, and the night
of love is a non-event. When Freddy preaches to Angela that this is

> one of those dark ages that visits mankind between millennia,
> between the death and rebirth of gods, when there is nothing to
> steer by but sex and stoicism and the stars.   (372/411)

she promptly falls asleep.

The final section of the novel, It's Spring Again, dramatises the
consequences of the social ethic in wider political and religious
terms. After Foxy's abortion, apparently safe at last, Piet attends
the Tarbox town meeting, a political gathering marked by easy
consensus and group passivity. Tarbox has now reached full
suburban status as each year more commuters move in to outlying
developments. The older inhabitants have been displaced by the
voting power of the new group, and incomers now hold positions
of power. The town attorney is an urbane Boston lawyer, who has
taken the job as a hobby; the moderator is a professor of sociology.
Even Piet's friends have joined the various town committees,
swallowed up in a suburban ethos of acquiescent participation.
Significantly, no real issues are debated. New schools, highways,
sewer bonds and zoning by-laws 'all smoothly slid by, greased by
federal grants' (386/428). Living democracy is failing, with
attendance at the meeting already perceived by some as an empty
charade. 'There was annual talk now of representative town
meeting, and the quorum had been halved' (387/428). Even the
location, the new high school, where the adjustable partitions
have ceased to adjust, bears witness to a code of social adjustment
which has ossified. Both Angela and Piet conform to the herd.
Angela, exhausted by daily commuting to a psychiatrist in
Boston, adds drowsy 'Ayes' to the unanimous crowd. Her

husband is bored by politics. 'Piet went to town meetings to see his friends' (387/429). On this occasion, however, nobody sits with the Hanemas, who are also excluded from the post-meeting drinks. As Piet subsequently discovers, Georgene has spilled the beans. Her motivation is ironically appropriate. After Foxy's abortion Georgene had cared for her, enjoying the 'domestic conspiracy' (381/421) of the two women. When she later finds Foxy and Piet together she feels betrayed and, adopting the role of outraged clubwoman, denounces the pair.

Summoned to the Whitmans' for a confrontation, Piet reacts much as if he were attending another group meeting, telling Angela that 'we're just here so that I can get reprimanded' (394/436). On arrival he notes that 'In the society of Tarbox there was no invitation more flattering than to share, like this, another couple's intimacy' (395/437). The confrontation cuts across the most cherished beliefs of the group. Ken, the scientist, discards Foxy on the grounds that 'there are reactions which are reversible and those that aren't. This feels irreversible' (399/441). Not all human situations can be adjusted or socially controlled. Piet is astonished to find that Ken does not view the situation as a four-sided problem 'equally shared' and has no intention of talking it out. When Ken announces his plan to bring criminal charges against Freddy, Piet's plea that Freddy acted out of love for his friends founders. Even as he pleads he recognises the futility of the argument. 'He was loyal to the God Who mercifully excuses us from pleading. Who nails his joists of judgment down firm, and roofs the universe with order' (399/441). From this point on Freddy's evangelical humanism no longer threatens Piet. When Angela throws him out he reverts to an older creed, recognising, 'Behind the screen of couples and houses and days a Calvinist God' (415/459). Freddy's attempt to operate as secular priest, in the name of love and mercy, and in the ostensible interests of the group, reveals the fraudulence of the group ethic. Excluded, entirely alone, Piet is left to reflect that he misses Foxy less than adultery itself, 'its adventure, the acrobatics its deceptions demand, the tension of its hidden strings' (429/475).

The novel concludes with an incident which has vexed more than one critic, the burning of the Congregational church, with its apocalyptic overtones. Tension is a key concept here. On the beach with his daughters, Piet notes a 'herd-like' crowd (439/486), trapped between dunes and sea, listening to 'love and peace' music. 'Then the supernatural proclaimed itself' (439/486). In a sudden storm, lightning strikes the church, which burns to the ground. The crowd watch, uncomprehending, in disbelief that the fire and the torrential rain can exist together, 'as if a conflict in God's heart had been bared' (443/490). Although Piet rejoices, in gratitude at having been shown 'something beyond him, beyond all blaming' (443/491), it is important to note that what is beyond him is not some easy answer or bolt of relevation, but a conflict, a tension of rain and fire. The description makes both a theological and a social point, suggesting that (to draw on Fromm) social conformism is incompatible with Christianity. Inasmuch as God is unrecognisable, indefinable, a conflict, inasmuch as man is made in his image, man is indefinable which means that he is not a thing manipulable according to social laws. The terms of the description also indicate the inadequacies of the attenuated Tarbox creed. However much the firemen attempt to water it down the fire thrives on the architectural hollowness of the building, feeding on the empty spaces between walls, roof and ceiling. Of the structure only the weathervane survives, a small cock with a penny for an eye, an apt symbol of the erotic hedonism of the group, of their church which has abandoned fixed principles to shift with the winds of social change, and of their commercial orientation. When the Reverend Pedrick waylays Piet as 'a man of the world' (444/492) to enquire about restoration costs, Piet has his revenge on the businessman preacher, reeling out punitive percentages and figures. When Pedrick rephrases Freddy's belief, that the church is not just a building, but 'people, human beings' (444/492) Piet tells him in return that only total demolition is feasible. In the event the church turns out to be not only badly gutted but so structurally unsound that it might well have collapsed without the fire. Rumour has it that the new church will be, not a restoration, but a poured concrete tent-shape, an appropriate structure for the flimsy beliefs of Tarbox. Foxy's letters point towards the moral. In the Virgin Islands Foxy has begun to attend a Lutheran church, where she finds the sermons intellectually challenging. She has also met people who care about 'international affairs, if that's what they are. I've forgotten what else "affair" means' (448/496). She comes to the conclusion that Kennedy 'wasn't fit to rule us, which is to say we aren't fit to rule ourselves, so bring on emperors, demi-gods, giant robots' (449/496).

Whether Piet and Foxy can act upon their new-found knowledge remains, however, distinctly unlikely. In the mock-Victorian parcelling out of fates at the end, Foxy and Piet recede into the distance. Piet sells his interest in the firm, marries Foxy, and takes a job with the largest and most conformist of organisations, becoming a construction inspector of military barracks. The pair move to Lexington

> where, gradually, among people like themselves, they have been accepted as another couple. (458/506)

This sting in the tail of the novel consigns the pair to a diminished fate, distancing them from the reader. Though marriage to Foxy is a 'happy ending' for Piet, happiness has become a questionable concept. Updike's own comments on him suggest reservations:

> He becomes merely a name in the last paragraph; he becomes a satisfied person and in a sense dies. In other words, a person who has what he wants, a satisfied person, a content person, ceases to be a person. Unfallen Adam is an ape. . . . I feel that to be a person is to be in a situation of tension, is to be in a dialectical situation. A truly adjusted person is not a person at all. (*Picked-Up Pieces* p. 504)

3

The World of Work: *Rabbit, Run, Rabbit Redux* and *Rabbit Is Rich*

Published at roughly ten-year intervals, the novels which constitute the *Rabbit* trilogy (*Rabbit, Run* (1960), *Rabbit Redux* (1971), *Rabbit Is Rich* (1982)) appear to differ somewhat in their major emphases (respectively religious, political and economic). As Updike has also announced his intention to complete a tetralogy, critical discussions of the overall form of the work must inevitably remain tentative. None the less, the trilogy coheres internally around one major organising theme: that of the relation between individual and society, particularly expressed as the instinctual, sensual and libidinous dimensions of the human being in conflict with social constraints which are politically and economically determined. Freud's analysis of society as founded upon repression is important in this connection, though Updike is no naive Freudian and clearly contests Freud's understanding of religious faith as an illusion. For Freud the methodical sacrifice of libido to work and reproduction *is* culture. Because the lasting inter-personal relations on which civilisation depends presuppose that the sex instincts are inhibited, there is therefore a fundamental opposition between sex and social utility, and a high price in individual happiness which must be paid for the benefits of civilised life. Most work requires that energy be directed away from direct sexual satisfaction, to produce the gains of technical civilisation, a process arguably exacerbated in modern society in which desire is over-controlled ('surplus repression') in order to maintain men as cogs in the industrial machine. In the trilogy Updike introduces this central conflict in *Rabbit, Run*, proceeding in *Rabbit Redux* to examine the potential sensual liberation of the individual, freed from toil by the new technology, and finally in *Rabbit Is Rich*, analysing the ways in which society may deform and exploit the instincts by the creation of mass fantasy, in order to repress once more. Work, technology and sex are therefore the three major strands braided together throughout the trilogy.

Updike's original plan for *Rabbit, Run* envisaged its publication in one volume with *The Centaur*, as companion novellas, illustrating, in the contrast of running rabbit and plodding horse, the polarity 'between the life of instinctual gratification and that of dutiful self-sacrifice' (*Hugging the Shore*, p. 849). Updike has also stated that 'I do buy Freud's notion about the radical centrality of sex', but moved on in the same interview to argue that what has radical centrality for his characters is work:

> My novels are all about the search for useful work. So many people these days have to sell things they don't believe in and have jobs that defy describing.[12]

Harry 'Rabbit' Angstrom's job, selling the MagiPeel peeler, clearly fits the description. In *Rabbit, Run*, Rabbit rebels against the constraints of his society, taking off on an impulsive flight from his domestic responsibilities (his wife Janice and son Nelson) to indulge his sexual instincts with Ruth Leonard. In Freudian terms, nature and culture are irrevocably in opposition. Rabbit's hostility to his society therefore finds expression in a quasi-romantic return to nature – in his original fugue into the countryside, his outdoor walks with Ruth and his new job as a gardener. As Gerry Brenner[13] has established, this return to nature is treated critically in the action of the novel, in which society apparently emerges victorious. Rabbit's opposition to his culture also finds expression (as Brenner has also noted) in the pervasive imagery of society as net, web or trap in which the individual is entangled and caught. More generally, critical interest has focused upon the character of Rabbit, who has been seen as social rebel, malefactor, existential quester, anti-hero, saint and scoundrel. The central problem here, that of Rabbit's 'immaturity', also derives from the Freudian opposition. Is Rabbit immature in the sense of being irresponsible, selfish and damaging to others? Or is there a sense in which he stands for values of presocial innocence, instinct, even spiritual grace, which are lost to social man? Here it is worth noting Updike's own comments upon the hero, which underline his intentions in respect of other choric protagonists. For Updike, the very idea of a hero is an aristocratic and therefore outmoded notion. 'Now either nobody is a hero or everyone is. I vote for everyone.'[14] Though Rabbit is the central figure in the novel, his fate has general implications. Quite apart from his representative status as an average Middle-American, he is surrounded by other characters (particularly Eccles and Janice) equally engaged in the attempt to get back to an instinctive and infantile existence, whose internal monologues provide access to the deeper levels of their unconscious thoughts.

Opposed understandings of childishness also condition the form of the novel. In his nickname, buck teeth, destructive rampages and libidinous nature, Harry is modelled upon Peter Rabbit,[15] transplanted to the flower-pot red brick city of Brewer. Where Peter Rabbit frames Harry within a tale of innocent animality, a second work for children implies the reverse. At several points in the novel Eccles refers to Hilaire Belloc's double volume for children, *The Bad Child's Book of Beasts and Cautionary Tales for Children*. Joyce Eccles has been frightened by the lion, in 'Jim – Who Ran Away from his Nurse and was Eaten by a Lion'. The volume also contains the tale of Rebecca (Who Slammed Doors for Fun and Perished Miserably), a shadowy proleptic image of the fate of Rabbit's daughter. This opposition between fable and frightening cautionary tale, between indulgent celebration of instinct and its repression, lies at the heart of the novel, in which parents and children, innocence and animality are recurrent motifs.

In the first movement of the novel the marginalisation of sex by work is explicitly highlighted. Originally Harry and Janice met at work, at Kroll's Department Store, which they both detested: 'Every employee hated Kroll's' (13/13). On their release from work Janice and Harry rush straight to a friend's apartment to make love. Janice Springer's pregnancy, however, springs the marital trap. In the opening pages of the novel Rabbit arrives home to the clutter and confinement of his apartment, and to a Janice no longer pretty. *He* fantasises that 'tomorrow she'll be his girl again' (7/8). Although *she* is engrossed in a children's programme on TV, it ends with the injunction 'We must work, boys and girls. . . . That's the way to be happy' (9/9). Despatched to collect Nelson from his own parents, Rabbit observes his son through the window, in *his* former place at the table, and flees in horror from this image of eternal, repressive repetition. Ironically, however his flight is circular, returning him to Brewer. The return to childhood which he seeks, indicated in his nostalgia for his days as an adolescent basketball star, propels him towards Tothero, his old coach. Tothero is delighted to be reunited with one of his 'boys'. (He particularly enjoys watching Rabbit undress, which takes him back to locker-room days.) Drifting into sleep in Tothero's bed, Rabbit's mind moves from memories of the women he has 'nailed', to the 'factory-looking' (45/39) whores in Texas, and thence to the clamour of a neighbouring 'body shop' (46/40).

The implicit subordination of sex to industrial purposes is amplified in the character of Ruth Leonard, to whom Tothero introduces Rabbit. Initially Rabbit is attracted to Ruth, who seems 'good-natured' and who does 'Nothing' (62/52) – she does not work. In his first sexual encounter with her he clutches at an illusion of a return to innocence. In addition to treating her as a fantasy lover, he also converts her into a child, insisting on undressing her, scrubbing her face vigorously and even overseeing her in the toilet where, out of habit (he is toilet-training Nelson) he praises her performance warmly. Ironically, however, Ruth is a prostitute and Rabbit is paying for his illusions. What is play for him is work for Ruth. Though a real tenderness develops between the couple, subsequent events indicate Rabbit's inability to escape his social conditioning. In her interior monologue Ruth had remembered the oral–genital contacts of her trade as 'harder work than they [men] probably think, women are always working harder than they think' (146/118). Though Ruth abandons prostitution to become a stenographer, Harry eventually converts her back into a whore. Irritated by an encounter with Ronnie Harrison, one of Ruth's former men, Rabbit forces Ruth to perform fellatio once more, just as she did for her customers. When Harry is called away to Janice (in labour), Ruth's silence marks the couple's separation. Rabbit's flight has ended merely in a recreation of his original situation. He has converted sex into work, and sprung the trap on another – for unknown to him Ruth is pregnant too.

Although the initial excursion from responsibilities appears to have ended as a triumph for society, the conflict between innocent instincts and social responsibility is subsequently recast in religious terms, as the opposition between faith and good works.

During his absence from home Rabbit has been befriended by the Reverend Eccles, whose particular brand of religion concentrates upon good works and social busyness. Despite his creed, Eccles is regressively boyish. Though ostensibly intent upon reuniting Harry and Janice, he also profits from Harry's availability as a golf partner. As he admits, it is difficult for him to find men to play with: 'Everybody works except me' (107/88). Escaping to the course, he tells his wife, 'Don't think this is pleasure for me. It's work' (123/101). Lucy is unimpressed, aware that Jack enjoys giggling with his teenage parishioners about petting, or accompanying the young people's softball team to matches, in preference to spending time with his wife and daughters. Though Rabbit's return to Janice is a matter for congratulation for Eccles, Rabbit's own initial stand for grace and innocence (127/103) finds support in an unexpected quarter. When Eccles consults Kruppenbach, a Lutheran pastor, Kruppenbach makes it clear that Eccles is avoiding his real responsibilities (to be an exemplar of faith, (171/138)) in favour of ethical and social meddling. In Kruppenbach's tirade, the repeated phrase 'your job' simultaneously parodies Eccles's concern with good works (as a cover for play, and an escape from his religious duty) and also undercuts the social sacralisation of work:

> Do you think this is your job, to meddle in these people's lives? I know what they teach you at seminary now: this psychology and that. . . . You think now your job is to be an unpaid doctor, to run around and plug up the holes and make everything smooth. I don't think that. I don't think that's your job. (170/137)

The expansion of the central theme from that of nature versus society to that of faith versus good works establishes the conflict at the heart of the novel in a wider perspective, and illuminates later events.

For Harry, his return to Janice marks a reassumption of social duties. Though he now takes over parental responsibility, caring for Nelson while Janice is recovering, he is less happy with his new employment as a car salesman. The job is 'easy enough, if it isn't any work for you to lie' (234/190). Effectively he has swapped places with Janice. On his departure Janice had returned to her childhood home, where she consigned Nelson to the care of her parents in order to enjoy afternoons at the movies giggling with a former schoolfriend. When Rabbit meets Janice again in hospital she is high on pethidine, and full of uninhibited suggestions. On his next visit, however, he and Janice watch a television programme, 'Queen for a Day', in which people are financially rewarded for their personal unhappiness – an apt image of the workings of society. The domestic tragedies of the programme also point forward to the catastrophe of the novel, the accidental drowning of Rebecca by Janice. This event is very carefully designed by Updike to dramatise the central antithesis of the novel.

On the one hand the death suggests that repression is necessary to safeguard the innocent from the dangers of the instincts. Janice drowns Rebecca in part because she is hopelessly drunk. Befuddled, half naked and surrounded by domestic chaos, Janice regresses to a state of childish irresponsibility. (Part of her binge is spent crayoning with Nelson.) The mother's childishness thus destroys the actual child. Since Janice's binge is the result of Harry's second flight, his sexual instincts are also implicated. Harry runs because Janice refuses to permit sexual contact. He has been sexually ignited by Lucy, Eccles's come-hither wife, an amateur psychologist for whom faith is an illusion, and Christianity 'a very neurotic religion' (240/195). On this level, the death scene suggests that the free play of the instincts can lead only to disaster.

Things are, however, decidedly more complicated, as the proleptic television programme indicates. The sexual encounter between Harry and Janice founders upon thoughts of work. Grinding against her body, Harry feels that 'the whole sweet thing is just sweat and work' (247/200), while Janice is repelled by his practised motions and apparent pride in 'what a good job he was doing' (251/203). Rebecca's death is also multiply motivated. Eccles blames himself, for having brought the couple back together in the first place (266/215). Janice's drunkenness is also fed by her fear of social shame (her neighbours will laugh at her). Even Janice's father accepts a degree of blame, for not having made Janice feel securely loved (273/221). Janice had given the baby her mother's name in the hope that this would 'settle' her mother but 'instead it brings her mother against her breast' (250/202). Through her drunken haze Janice is continually aware of a shadowy third person watching her actions, an unseen presence which at first seems parental. An aside from Updike may be relevant here. 'If Freud is to be believed, we spend our emotional lives vainly seeking, amid a crowd of phantoms, to placate our parents' ghosts' (*Picked-Up Pieces*, p. 289). In fact a series of phone calls from parents leads directly to disaster. Harry's absence from the workplace is noticed by Mr Springer, who phones Janice and then alerts his wife. It is the prospect of Mrs Springer's disapproval at the chaos of the apartment which propels Janice into bathing Rebecca. Had she simply wallowed in drink, Rebecca would have lived. Here the attempt to placate the mother destroys the child; the reassumption of social responsibility proves as dangerous to the innocent as its abandonment. Even the time scheme of events is significant. On Sunday, released from work, Rabbit's instincts reassert themselves and he runs. On Monday, as the workday dawns, Janice reassumes her duties and provokes catastrophe.

Thus far responsibility for Rebecca's death may be ascribed to Janice, Harry, Eccles, Lucy, parents, instincts or society. Only Harry sees through the welter of multiple causation to another responsible party – God. Draining the bathwater he thinks, 'how easy it was, yet in all his strength God did nothing. Just that little rubber stopper to lift' (276/224). Janice herself, in her frenzied attempts at resuscitation, prays as if 'clasping the knees of a vast third person whose name, Father, Father, beats against her head' (264/214). Society, however, swiftly mobilises to eclipse this fleeting recognition of a power beyond itself. Tothero assures Harry that 'Right and wrong aren't dropped from the sky. We. We make them' (279/226). Eccles, even more crashingly insensitive, congratulates Harry on the possibility that the disaster has reunited him in guilt with Janice, and further rejoices in the vindication of his 'good works' theory: 'We must work for forgiveness; we must *earn* the right to see that thing [God] behind everything' (281/227). Everyone behaves as if the death is Harry's fault, as the group collaborate to make the father the scapegoat and guilty party.

Temporarily Harry and Janice conform to the social group. At Rebecca's funeral both characters appear in parental clothing. Harry is wearing Mr Springer's shirt. Janice, in her mother's dress, is also engulfed in Mrs Angstrom's embrace. At the graveside, however, Harry rebels. He is in no doubt of Rebecca's resurrection (hardly the result of good works or faith) by a merciful God. His shocking speech, 'Don't look at *me*. I didn't kill her' (293/238), represents a fragile truth which is being vigorously obscured in the name of group cohesion. Tearing off Springer's shirt Rabbit runs once more for the dark forest. The scene suggests a deliberate undercutting of Freud's belief (in the fiction of the primal crime, parricide) that society is based upon shared guilt. By choosing the death of an innocent child, rather than that of the primal father, Updike foregrounds the horrible price of social cohesion, its delusory basis, and the patricentric nature of the Freudian idea. Throughout the novel fathers figure as ineffectual authorities. The authoritarian father of the Freudian model is distinctly lacking. Tothero enjoys masochistic humiliation from girlfriend and wife, Eccles is bullied by wife and daughters, Mr Angstrom Senior is dominated by his wife, and Mrs Springer inspires considerably more fear than her husband. This demystification of male authorities reinforces the sense in which the novel benefits from Freud's insights, while simultaneously providing a critique. As Lucy puts it, 'Freud is like God; you make it true' (117/96). In the civilisation of the Fifties the repressive father has been edged out, replaced by society itself which now acts directly upon the individual. At the close of the novel Harry discovers Ruth's pregnancy and finds himself caught in a double-bind. His flight to Ruth has been a contributory factor in the death of Rebecca. If, however, he abandons Ruth once more for his established responsibilities she will abort the expected child. Faced with this irreconcilable conflict Rabbit takes off once more. The novel ends in the present with Rabbit in motion: 'he runs. Ah: runs. Runs' (307/249). Throughout the novel the use of the present tense contributes to the impression of characters living in the thoughtless immediacy of the instincts. It also, however, has another function, to evoke the mass media and thus to catch Rabbit within a social frame. Updike originally intended to subtitle the novel 'A Movie'. 'The present tense was in part meant to be an equivalent of the cinematic mode of narration' (*Picked-Up Pieces*, p. 496). When Rabbit reappears, in *Rabbit Redux* and *Rabbit Is Rich*, the media figure prominently, in the former novel as potentially liberating, in the latter as delusory and repressive.

Rabbit Redux has sparked considerable interest as a more overtly political novel than its predecessors. Set between 16 July and October 1969, it incorporates references to the Apollo moon shot, the rise of the 'alternative' culture, civil rights protests and

Chappaquiddick, among other events in the news. The somewhat stereotyped characters of black activist Skeeter and flower-child Jill also suggest a novel with a political intention. Most critics have, however, remained uncertain as to the status of historical events within the novel, which also includes a cluster of image patterns which suggest a more ahistorical spatial form, and a cyclic structure in which Harry Angstrom's excursion into a different world, on his wife's flight, appears to lead him nowhere. As a result more than one reader has remained uncertain where the primary focus lies. Do the historical events occupy the foreground of the novel, acting upon representative characters who are swayed by large social forces? Or are they merely symbolic background, extensions of Harry Angstrom's subjective sense of self? It is my contention that, far from being a weakness in the novel, this uncertainty is deliberately fostered by Updike in order to explore the relation between medium and message. In this connection the content of particular news items is less important than the fact that Harry is continually bombarded by them. Robert Detweiler has perceptively identified Harry with Marshall McLuhan's 'Gutenberg man', thus drawing attention to a dimension of the novel which deserves further development. Arguably, although *Rabbit Redux* explores a variety of political issues, it subordinates them, in the final analysis, to a larger theme, that of technological evolution and its consequences, with special reference to the theories of Marshall McLuhan.

Marshall McLuhan's theorisation of the role of the media in Western culture resists easy summary, containing its own contradictions and shifts of emphasis.[16] Essentially, however, McLuhan understands a medium as an extension of one or more of our senses, the telephone extending the sense of hearing, the camera that of sight. For McLuhan 'the medium is the message', the whole manner in which a particular medium disseminates information is more important than any particular message. Thus the primary influence of television is not in its content (screen violence, for example) but in the way its whole nature changes people's mental attitudes and habits of perception. McLuhan's analysis develops from an idiosyncratic historical overview of ways in which technology has affected us. Believing that human beings only function at their full potential if all their senses interact with their cultural environment, he argues that since the invention of printing by Gutenberg in the fifteenth century,

Western culture has been slavishly dominated by the eye, with a consequent impoverishment of the other senses. Complex patterns of oral communication (which might involve gesture, facial expression, touch, sound and sight), handcrafted texts and illuminated manuscripts yield to the uniform book the intellectual property of its author, rather than the expression of a communal tradition. The solitary human being now reads silently and individually, isolated in the sensory poverty of print. In addition, because printing ensures that communication can survive undistorted through time and space, society is able to maintain and prolong political identity and bureaucratic control. The printed book therefore ushers in a social and political system which destroys the communal order of the medieval or tribal world, and promotes competitive individualism under state control. Mechanical, linear typography is thus credited, somewhat monocausally, with the rise of Nationalism, the Reformation, Newtonian science and the Industrial Revolution. In particular the visual uniformity of print constitutes a primitive model of industrial technology. Mechanical type mechanises the word, breaking up experience into uniform units. The book, therefore, an early example of the mass-produced, uniformly repeatable commodity, disposes men towards repeatable and standardised patterns of organisation, homogenising culture in the process. The man who is conditioned by print willingly submits to timetables, lists and mass-production procedures. Gutenberg man is therefore logical, literal and individual, isolated from full sensual experience, and emotionally detached from his peers.

In McLuhan's theory the rise of the new electronic media (television, telephone, radio, film, the computer) reverses this process, connecting cities and countries instantaneously and creating a 'global village'. Human solidarity is fostered, with a consequent return to tribal unity on a world scale. For the individual, the new media offer a richer aesthetic experience, simultaneously involving different senses and creating a participatory effect. McLuhan distinguishes between 'hot' media and their 'cool' alternatives. 'Hot' media (e.g. the realist novel) provide plenty of data; the passive reader does not need to participate by filling in details. 'Cool' media (e.g. the telephone) provide little data and imagination has to fill in the gaps. In addition, the new media offer reconciliation between elite and

popular forms. Just as Cubism fosters the idea that the world
cannot be considered from one point of view, providing
simultaneous imaginative options, so the 'front-page Cubism' of
the newspaper, in which ads, photos, cartoons and news items
contend for attention, undermines linear and sequential patterns.
In this optimistic scenario, fragmented Western man is now
transformed into a complex depth-structured person, sensually
reintegrated, and emotionally aware of his interdependence with
human society. In *Understanding Media* McLuhan categorises his
typographic man as 'The Ugly American', referring to the title of
a novel by Eugene Burdick and William J. Lederer (1958) which
highlights the incomprehension of visually-oriented Americans
when confronted with the rich auditory and tribal cultures of the
east. In contrast the electronic media are conducive to
retribalisation. Where previously members of minority social
groups (McLuhan cites the Negro and the teenager) were
invisible, all social groups now interpenetrate and all cultures
become part of our lives.

Inevitably this Utopian blueprint has had its critics.
'McLuhanacy' (John Fekete's coinage) fails to take account of the
dangers of the media as drug, promoting electronically induced
mass-psychosis, and susceptible to state control. (McLuhan's
own research attracted funds from computer companies and the
US government.) McLuhan's variant slogan, 'the medium is the
massage', itself highlights the ability of the media to work us over
completely, reducing human beings to docile servo-mechanisms
of the machine. As Jonathan Miller noted, McLuhan is really a
sophisticated Luddite with a concealed 'burning of the books'
message, which is influenced by his own Catholic and Agrarian
ideology. In his cyclic model of history, technology is cast as a
second fall of man, with printing as the new original sin. Looking
back to an idealised Golden Age, McLuhan heralds the electronic
media as salvation, culminating in a renewed collectivity, a
catholic vision of all men as members, if not of one church, at least
of one global community.

While one might expect Updike, as a Protestant as well as a
writer of books, to reject the inherent secularisation of religious
vision implicit in McLuhan's thought, in fact he has applauded
McLuhan for his 'willingness to see possibility where others see
only doom' (*Picked-Up Pieces*, p. 484). In 1969, reflecting on 'The
Future of the Novel' in what he described as 'an age of

McLuhanism', Updike conceded that the new electronic age threatened to 'dull our sensibilities and eclipse our humanistic heritage' (*Picked-Up Pieces*, p. 18) but was none the less attracted to the innovative aesthetic potential of that age. Pointing to concrete poetry, Egyptian hieroglyphics and illuminated manuscripts as positive examples of accommodation among eye-oriented media, he went on to suggest new possibilities for the novel:

> The surface of the page, now a generally dead rectangle of gray, a transparent window into the action, could be a lively place of typographic invention . . . a surface that says, "This is printing." (*Picking-Up Pieces*, p. 22)

In *Rabbit Redux* Updike puts these new possibilities to the test, both in thematic and formal terms. Thematically the novel examines the concept of the 'global village', bringing its typographic hero into contact with a wider world of minority groups, social protest and foreign politics, presented through a succession of experiences in different media. Updike's own medium, however, is at least as important as his message. The novel employs a variety of different typographies, together with doodles, ideograms, and pictorial signs, and highlights a series of highly individualised languages, and character voices. The cyclic structure of McLuhan's thought comes under examination, while Updike also strikes variations on McLuhan's own hot/cool terminology in a cluster of image patterns which continually question technological values.

In the first section of the novel, *Pop/Mom/Moon*, Updike carefully establishes Harry Angstrom as Gutenberg Man, sensually deprived and passively dependent upon the machine. A social conformist and ardent supporter of state intervention in Vietnam, Harry lives his life by outdated rules, values order and neatness, and is isolated from his fellows to the point of racism. Sex has lost its charms for him, he no longer plays contact sports, and exists in a standard suburban locale on a diet of ersatz TV dinners. Stooped by a decade as a linotyper, Harry appears in the opening scene with 'a weakness verging on anonymity' (4/9). Confronted by Pop's news of Janice's adultery, Harry adopts two diversionary strategies to avoid getting the message, each of them linked to technology. Initially Harry turns away from the sound of Pop's voice towards the soundless image on the TV screen, repeatedly broadcasting the Apollo moon shot. Profoundly unmoved, Harry shares his reaction with the other drinkers: 'They have not been lifted, they are left here' (7/12). In a second programme, quiz-show entrants contend for an eight-foot frozen-food locker. Together with the iced drinks and air-conditioned chill of the bar, the pervasive cold imagery suggests a parallel with the state of human beings, as emotionally frozen, left behind by the new technology. Harry's father, however, also a printer, glories in technology, seeing himself as one of the little men who have been 'a piece of grit in the launching pad' (11/16). When Harry turns the conversation once more away from Janice towards his mother's illness, Pop declares his faith in medical technology. According to him, Mom should 'put herself in deep freeze' (8/13), until scientists discover a miracle cure. Harry is less optimistic, reflecting ironically upon the fact that Pop, the anonymous little man, survives, while Mom, 'the source of his life' (12/16), is failing. The two remaining members of Harry's family are also dwarfed by the machine. Back home Harry listens with one ear to Nelson extolling the delights of Billy's new machines (hi-fi and mini-bike) and takes refuge in television. When Janice puts in an appearance, Harry reaches out to caress her, but thinks instead of 'feathering the linotype keys, of work tomorrow, and is already there' (27/29). Tactility, emotional closeness, oral communication yield to the attractions of the machine and the demands of the working timetable.

At the Brewer *Vat*, a conservative rag specialising in racial innuendo, crime stories and jingoism, Harry is seen setting an item with also celebrates technology: BREWER FACTORY TOOLS COMPONENT HEADED TOWARDS MOON. Carefully rearranging the spaces and columns of the item to avoid a 'widow', an awkward gap in the lines, Harry revels in the warmth of the press's hot-lead processes. The machine appears here as if eroticised, able to meet all the individual's emotional needs. It stands, warm and 'mothering' above him. It is also described as a baby (30/31). Unlike Harry's own child its demands are few and once they are met 'obedience automatically follows' (31/31). With the machine, in contrast to Janice, 'there is no problem of fidelity. Do for it, it does for you' (31/31). Accosted once more by Pop at the coffee-break, Harry is grateful to return to the machine, personified here as 'pleased he is back' (31/33). Mother, wife, child, the all-enclosing machine 'fits right around him' (31/33). While the message Harry sets celebrates the new electronic technology (the machine part is in the space rocket's navigation computer) Harry remains trapped within the mental set of typographic attitudes: obedience, docility, dependence.

When watching television with Nelson, Harry had enjoyed a comic skit in which the Lone Ranger's wife, disenchanted with her husband's concentration on his work, takes Tonto as a lover. While Harry ignores the obvious parallels with his own situation, he is momentarily drawn to consider Tonto as a member of an oppressed minority. Rather in McLuhanite terms he speculates on Tonto as a Judas to his tribe. Whereas in the past he had accepted that Tonto was simply on the side of right, that law and order belonged to the white man, Harry is now much less certain. 'Where has the side of right gone?' he wonders. When, however, he figures as Paleface to Stavros's Tonto, in the ensuing scene in the Greek restaurant, Harry reverts to type. Janice characterises Harry and Nelson as 'Ugly Americans', insular, imperialistic and hostile to other cultures. Harry notes only that Janice and Stavros are sitting too close together 'to his printer's sense' (48/47), leaving awkward space on either side of them and creating a 'widow'. In the ensuing argument over Vietnam, described here as 'one more Cherokee uprising' (49/48), Harry defends America as order, opposed to darkness and chaos, and as a source of technological bounty. Stavros sums up his view of American benevolence in an image which associates America, Mom and the mothering machine: 'We're the big mama trying to make this unruly kid take some medicine' (46/45). While Janice and Stavros linger over delicious Greek food, Harry and Nelson are impatient to see *2001: A Space Odyssey*, a film which also celebrates technological evolution. Stavros is uninterested: 'I don't find technology all that sexy' (42/42). In the event the film also makes little impact on the Angstroms. Eclipsed by the confirmation of Janice's adultery it merely numbs them (51/49), providing a means of avoiding emotional confrontation.

Where Harry seems to be stranded in the typographic world, Janice's affair with Stavros appears to open up new vistas. The Greek restaurant with its tasty food, handwritten menus and extended Greek family in the background suggests possibilities of sensual reintegration and social retribalisation. Harry has already noted Janice's use of Stavros's slang, hearing 'another voice in hers' (20/23). When Stavros arrives in the restaurant Janice also adopts a new set of theatrical gestures (41/41). On her return from the movie, Janice lies awake, masturbating beside Harry. Her long interior monologue, verging on stream-of-consciousness, is non-sequential, free-flowing and centred, somewhat evidently, on feelings. For Janice, what originally attracted her to Stavros was than he allowed her to tumble out her thoughts in any way (53/51) as opposed to Harry, whom she sees as rule-bound. Compared with the sensual intensity of her love affair, the rest of her life now appears like 'a movie, flat and even rather funny' (53/51). As the reference to electronic technology suggests, the opposition between sensual Janice and deadened Harry is not, however, entirely clear-cut. While ostensibly rejecting the work ethic, celebrating her body as sexual plaything, Janice also mentally accuses Harry for not having awakened her sensuality, on the grounds that 'It was his job to call it out' (56/54). Irony cuts both ways here. When Janice loses concentration she thinks in terms of getting on with the job in hand: 'This is silly. This thinking is getting nowhere' (56/54). Ominously, in her sexual encounters with Stavros, Janice often relies on a mental image of Mom to provoke orgasm. In addition her comment here on her solitary orgasm, 'it's always best when you do it to yourself' (56/54), suggests sensual isolation rather than integration. When Harry finally confronts her, Janice attempts to fend him off with the terms of her working vocabulary – bills of lading, customs forms, franchises – just as she had earlier used 'working late' as a cover for play.

Janice's eventual confession seems at first to confirm Harry's earlier intuition that 'the news isn't all in, a new combination might break it open, this stale peace' (6/11). For a moment cracks appear in the cut-and-dried surface of Harry's life. Janice makes him see that 'there were rules beneath the surface rules which also mattered' (68/63). Yet though the couple now make love several times in the light, the visual and mechanical emphasis remains relentless. Janice celebrates daylight love ('Don't you love seeing?' (69/65)), but in the event their sexual encounters are illuminated by a soundless TV set, flickering bluish images across them, transforming Janice into desert sand, Harry into 'a barren landscape lit by bombardment' (70/65). Janice's hasty touches are subordinate to the 'flickering touch' of the set. The fragile possibility of a new development in their relationship collapses under the threat of the visual. Harry is aghast to discover that rumours are flying: 'It's all over town. Talk about daylight' (73/68). His fear of exposure to the power of the eye is vividly suggested when he imagines that his news will be headlined in the *Vat*: LINOTYPER'S WIFE LAYS LOCAL SALESMAN. Passively, he hands Janice over to Stavros, 'as long as I don't have to see the bastard' (78/72). Turning away from Janice's scrawled farewell note, Harry picks up the phone book and searches out

Stavros Chas 1204EisenhwerAv.

Rather than telephone, however, he contemplates this different typographic item, 'as if to see his wife, smaller than a pencil dot, crawling between the letters' (86/79). Print still dominates Harry's perceptions, and he remains trapped within the domination of the eye.

Consigning his wife and her lover to the printed item, Harry retreats into two excursions with parents, each of which draws attention to him as a figure in transition between two stages of technological development. The first, a baseball game attended with Janice's father, foregrounds the inevitability of Harry's evolution. For once the game bores him: 'the spaced dance of the men in white fails to enchant, the code . . . refuses to yield its meaning' (83/76). As a national ritual the game reflects McLuhan's theories. Harry notes that the players are 'specialists like any other' (83/77) in a game in which each player seems intent upon a 'private dream of making it' (83/77). In *Understanding Media* McLuhan analysed the reasons for the change in popularity in America, from baseball to football. Just as technologies are extensions of the animal organism, so games are extensions of social man. Their relative popularity reflects American social evolution, from baseball, an elegant image of a specialised, individualist society, to the new social centre, football, a non-positional and decentralised sport, in which players can switch to any role in the course of the game. Significantly, Nelson, who later takes up football, is unmoved by the baseball game, missing TV's running commentary and commercials.

From the outdated national ritual, Harry moves to a more personal celebration, Mom's birthday, which coincides with the triumph of new technology in the moon-landing. Contemplating an array of possible gifts in a drugstore, he discards a Sunbeam

Clipmaster and Roto-Shine Magnetic Electric Shoe Polisher, in favour of a Quikease Electric Massager. He comments that 'It is life. Life is a massage' (90/82). Evolving in response to technology, Harry appears to adopt the McLuhanite message in its least affirmative form. The entire final scene of the section amplifies the dehumanising consequences of the new technology. Far from becoming a global village, Brewer has been transformed into a ghost town; everyone is indoors watching the moon shot on television. Mom's appearance develops the impression of a sick, over-mechanised America. Her speech, disrupted by drugs, is no longer linear but robotic, broken up by random pauses. 'The doctor. Wants me up. I had to bake a cake. Earl wanted' (93/85). The reader has to remove the full-stops and reconnect the sentences to make any sense of her utterance. Her blank gaze reminds Harry of a 'blackboard from which they will all be wiped clean' (93/84), suggesting the loss of humanity involved in the loss of language. Unable to show Nelson any affection. Mom is reduced to massaging his head with the Quikease.

In the background the computerese banalities of the spacemen carry a similar message of human expression disintegrating and impoverished by technology. An astronaut speaks:

I was trying to get time sixteen sixty-five out and somehow it proceeded on the six-twenty-two before I could do a BRP thirty-two enter. (96/87)

Lost amidst references to torquing angles, recycling and gravity align, Harry finds that the technological terms make the voice quite incomprehensible. Nelson and Harry adopt space language themselves: 'We better rendezvous with our spacecraft.' 'Negative Pop.' (99/89) But they remain to watch the moon-landing only in order to avoid returning to their empty house. Nelson and Pop promptly sleep through the broadcast, while Harry misses the vital phrase 'one small step for a man, one giant leap for mankind', hearing only 'something about steps' (99/90) obscured by crackle. The medium in fact completely obscures the message, and the degree of viewer participation is minimal. Visually the TV screen provides data in excess, but the actual event, the spacewalk, seems no more real than preceding simulations, and electronic letters have to spell out that MAN IS ON THE MOON. Harry's final comment, as Mom massages his head refers equally to the moonshot and to Janice's flight: 'I know it's happened but I don't feel anything yet' (100/90). The section closes therefore on a note which suggests that old and new technologies are equally dehumanising, fostering similar degrees of dependence and emotional deadness. Harry remains poised between two alternative social and technological states, in each of which his identity is attenuated and his feelings benumbed.

Harry's feelings are to some extent reawakened in the second section of the novel, *Jill*, which examines two particular aspects of McLuhanism, the need for sensual reintegration on a human level, and the backward looking, essentially cyclic structure of McLuhan's thought. Initially the section involves a retreat from all technology, and especially from the primacy of the visual. At the beginning Harry recognises the dreary sameness of his repetitive existence: 'He was lying down to die, had been lying down for years. His body had been telling him to' (103/93). As a result he responds to two invitations, from Peggy and from Buchanan. Harry's encounter with Peggy signals the rejection of the visually dominated in comic terms. Repelled by her wall eye, Harry makes a polite comment on the view from her picture window, only to find that Peggy is offering a different vista, up her skirt. Peggy hates machines and invites Harry to consider that 'You think with your whole person' (110/98). To round out her message Peggy outlines Harry's shape in the air. Attracted, Harry steps into the body-shape she has drawn with her gestures and is rewarded by her gumdrop-textured kiss. The incipient sensual reintegration is immediately interrupted however by their two sons, squabbling over a broken machine, the minibike.

The mood broken, Harry hesitates over a synthetic Lunar Special in the dazzling brightness of Burger Bliss, but turns away to Jimbo's Friendly Lounge, a black bar which is presented as a dark, non-visual but intensely synaesthetic locale. Music flows here, against a background of 'tickled mutterings' and the 'liquid of laughter' (114/102). All Harry's senses are immediately engaged. He drinks a Stinger, and sucks slowly on a joint, shared with Babe, who caresses his hand until 'his mind is racing with his pulse' (116/104). Sounds are also foregrounded. Buchanan parodies Harry's linear, linotype expression, giving the syllables of the parody 'an odd ticking equality' (116/103), describing Harry as a former 'ath-e-lete', and 'expert lino-typist' at 'Ver-i-ty Press'. In contrast the black voices, richly textured in accent and slang, hint at hidden meanings below the surface, in particular their desire to pass Jill on to Harry on the grounds that she makes them too 'visible' (130/115) to the police. Under the influence of dope Harry feels himself expanding 'to include beyond Jimbo's the whole world with its polychrome races' (132/117). The recorded music of the jukebox yields to Babe's interconnected medley of show tunes, flowing into each other and into older songs from an earlier unmechanised America, running back through ragtime to the cyclical vision of time in the words of Ecclesiastes, 'A time to be born, a time to die' (125/111). The whole episode appears to celebrate both social and sensual reintegration, and a cyclic return to an orginal Golden Age. Although Harry also feels continually threatened at Jimbo's, he becomes less passive, and is able to turn to meet the threat of muggers on the bridge home. Where previously Harry had distanced his fears, tending to cast them mentally in imaginary headlines (AUTOPSY ORDERED IN FRIENDLY LOUNGE DEATH) he now faces up to the threat rather than retreating into automatic visual defence mechanisms. Appropriately the movie house in the background has replaced *2001* with *True Grit*, also a celebration of physical courage and of an older set of American values.

Jill's presence in the Angstrom home is also originally presented in positive terms, as marking a separate peace, a retreat from the mechanical, and a rekindling of the senses. Jill banishes TV, substituting guitar music and discussion. Her healthy cooking restores Harry's 'taste for life' (171/150) and she uses music and poetry to draw the family together. When Jill improvises the ballad of her life to guitar accompaniment, Harry is at first aloof ('Don't rhyme on my account') but finally drawn in to the oral performance, following Jill's 'Narrangansett Bay' with an 'olé', and applauding with Nelson (175/152). In the oral sex which follows Jill becomes responsive to Harry's touch, her deadened emotions also reawakening. Without multiplying examples, it is fairly clear that both parties are, in auditory, oral and tactile ways, being 'led back' or 'restored to health' in the figurative meaning of *redux*. The new sensuality even extends to Mom, whose latest drug, L-dopa, eroticises her, making her feel perpetually lovey-dovey.

In addition the fresh sensual reintegration is accompanied by a renewed religious emphasis, also couched in McLuhanite terms. Jill, now clean of drugs, had originally been attracted to them as a source of religious visions. She expounds a playful, non-utilitarian view of the cosmos, in which the planets 'don't have to be used for anything' (161/141). In strong contrast to the anonymous surroundings of the Angstrom home, Jill propounds a vision of man as 'a mechanism for turning things into spirit and spirit into things' (159/139). For her, man's best creations, whether artistic or technological, are not anonymous but personal, bearing the mark of the craftsman's feelings. She argues that the artist expresses 'whatever he feels when he makes his mark' (159/139) leaving his feelings exposed 'like fingerprints, like handwriting'. Significantly, her own note to Harry is signed, not with her name but with ideograms and drawings, reproduced as such in the text. While sceptical, Harry is not dismissive. Jill's new non-competitive ethic enables him to avoid confrontation with Stavros over Janice, and the machine also appears to be losing its dominance. Returning eagerly home from the press, Harry comes across a film crew making a movie in Brewer, notes their 'heightened reality' and registers his own existence critically as 'dim' (184/161).

Harry's peaceful evolution into a richer sensual and spiritual world does not go unchecked for long, however. Another typesetting scene strikes a sourer note, undercutting the preceding positive images of a return to older values, and emphasising the illusory quality of any such return. Harry is setting an item concerning local excavations which have uncovered artefacts from the past, from the wall murals of a speakeasy, to old pictorial signs and Indian arrowheads. The historical evolution of Brewer from Indian trading post, through a colonial period when George Washington slept there, to the first iron mines and industrialisation, is briefly sketched. While the item celebrates technological development in terms of an unchecked continuity, it is actually interrupted twice by the pressing demands of the present. It is time for the return to school, pleasantly envisaged by Harry as 'beginning again and reconfirming the order that exists' (193/168). Buchanan, however, approaches Harry in the coffee-break, and 'touches' him for twenty dollars, for his children's back-to-school expenses. A second interruption, from Janice, arranges for Nelson to buy new school clothes on Saturday, rather than visiting Valley Forge with Jill. When Harry finally returns to the machine he is so out of control that he garbles three lines and finally sets one complete line of gibberish. On one level the errors indicate that his working habits of order and control are being disrupted by his emotions, messing up the established order. On another the message (handcrafted artefacts, an idealised American past) is undercut by its medium, print. The boss's anger that Janice has phoned during working hours also draws attention to the fact that Harry's life is still structured in terms of the school timetable and work, his time segmented into coffee-breaks and work shifts. The two interruptions pointedly undercut any notion of beginning again or returning to an American Golden Age. Buchanan's touch is strictly commercial. Harry hands over twenty dollars in exchange for Jill, much as if his relation to the blacks was merely the equivalent of trading with the Indians. There is no going back to Valley Forge. Nelson will buy silk neckties instead. Harry is left silently contemplating the out-of-date calendar in the office, an image of his own situation. Jill's alternative culture, with its non-materialistic, sensual and idealistic overtones is too fragile to withstand the power of the established order. When Jill does visit Valley Forge, she returns, high on drugs, having noted only George Washington's sleeping pills.

The implicit suggestion that American idealism fails, delivering man to the drug and the machine, is developed and made explicit in the character of Mom. Though L-dopa has to some extent restored her health, it has also sapped her will. Mom relates a series of frightening dreams in which she feels crowded by things, sees her children as corpses, and finds a dead man in the icebox. In contrast, however, to these familiar images of emotional deadness amidst materialism, the worst of her dreams projects a McLuhanite nightmare of the future. In the dream, people are reduced to puddles on hospital tables, connected by tubes to machines with television patterns on them, while Pop rejoices in the background, as he had earlier rejoiced over health insurance: 'The government is paying for it all' (196/171). Mom's dream pictures human beings as docile servo-mechanisms of the new machines, which feed upon them under the aegis of the state. Harry's bitter comment, 'That's not a dream. That's how it is' (196/171), indicates how far he has progressed from his earlier belief in state and technological benevolence. At the same time Harry also distances himself from Mom, angrily rebutting her suggestion that he abandon Janice and Nelson, to get free. Mom is interested only in her son, the generation of the past. 'Her tyrant love would freeze the world' (197/171). From his earlier flight, in *Rabbit Run*, however, and from the death of his daughter, Harry has learned that 'Freedom means murder' (198/172). Unwillingly Harry recognises that change is inevitable. The clock cannot be turned back to a world without Nelson or Janice. Already the maples outside his parents' home have been mutilated to protect electric wires. The American individualist ethic now reminds Harry only of the death of John F. Kennedy, suggesting that his society offers only two alternatives, murderous freedom or passive, drugged well-being. Harry returns, however, to his responsibility, his son, noting in the background that the movie house is now playing *BUTCH CSSDY & KID*.

The section closes with a sexual encounter between Harry and Jill that effectively rings the knell of their relationship. Making love in front of the 'mother planet' of the TV screen, the pair figure as 'moonchild' and 'earthman', the space vocabulary and the presence of the electronic medium dramatising the extent to which they remain trapped within the machine. Jill is now actually 'spaced out' on drugs, and as a result her dilated pupils emphasise her enormous eyes. Eroticism fails here. Jill is described as 'an angry mechanic' (202/176) working to arouse Harry, who only manages to complete the act by imagining a machine in Jill's belly. The fragile separate peace of an alternative cultural settlement collapses with the return of Nelson, laden with the excessive purchases which Janice has charged to Harry. From now on, as Harry realises, 'It's war' (203/17). The phrase has a special relevance. In *War and Peace in the Global Village* McLuhan discusses the consequences of the damage done to the American sense of identity by the new technology, noting two specific reactions. In the first, 'rear-mirrorism', the past is re-emphasised in an attempt to recover the older self-image. Alternatively McLuhan envisages war as a reaction to a threatened sense of self, an attempt to reassert identity in new terms. On the failure of Jill's past-oriented values, the novel moves forward to explore this alternative possibility.

In the third section of the novel, *Skeeter*, the emphasis shifts from the individual and religious aspects of McLuhanism to its social and political implications, in particular the notion of renewed human solidarity in a media-created global village. Where Jill essentially looked back to an older set of values, Skeeter's historical theology turns the clock forward, towards apocalypse rather than Golden Age. Importantly, Skeeter is also cast in McLuhanite terms. When he describes the blacks as the future, 'We're what has been left out of the industrial revolution, so we are the next revolution' (235/203), he paraphrases McLuhan's belief that 'backward' or minority cultures, which do not have to retrain literate and mechanical minds into electronic workers, have an inherent advantage over the obsolete typographic states, and are thus the wave of the future. By sheltering Skeeter, a fugitive, Harry definitively breaks the rules and stands out against the law, which he now describes as serving only a ruling elite. Skeeter, a Vietnam veteran, also ends Harry's passivity, challenging him to fight, physically, and provoking a series of verbal confrontations. At the printing plant Harry is rewarded by the return of Buchanan's 'touch', and by Farnsworth's acknowledgment that they are 'brothers in paternity' (219/191). Cheered by his sense of interracial male brotherhood, Harry is able to slam the phone down on Janice's next interruption and to finish setting the type-item of this section without error.

In contrast to Jill, Skeeter reintroduces both books and television to the Angstrom home. In a series of structured discussions he puts the Angstroms through a short course in Afro-American history, with selected readings from his sacred texts. Skeeter obtained the books while serving in Vietnam, and his comment, 'They love us to read, that crazy Army' (226/197), connects linear reading with military regimentation. In *his* readings, however, the readers skip to and fro between different texts, and importantly they read aloud. Updike calls attention here to the personal voice, each distinctive, as opposed to the anonymity of print. Jill reads in an unnaturally high 'nice-girl-school' voice, Nelson stumbles over the words but slowly gains confidence. The readings shake the parody out of Skeeter's voice, while Harry reads 'thrillingly' (247/213) as a black. The reading ends with Skeeter's comment, 'Makes a pretty good nigger, don't he?' (247/214), as the four gather to watch *Laugh-In*. The television skit, in which black Sammy Davis and white Arne Johnson appear 'like one man looking into a crazy mirror' (247/214), reinforces the impression that Harry and Skeeter are brothers under the skin, brought together by the new medium.

For Updike's readers the typographic form of the readings also carries its own messages. The selections are set in smaller italicised type, squashing more words to the line and creating a cramped and old-fashioned impression, in marked contrast to the more spacious typography in which the main events of the novel are set. Where the preceding sections were largely divided into uniform sub-sections, the *Skeeter* section substitutes a series of unconnected scenes, separated by asterisks, undated and of variable length. Less clearly sequential, these short sections undermine the earlier realist texture of the novel, suggesting a less linear reading and inviting Updike's readers to make connections for themselves.

Skeeter's own monologues explicitly recognise the deficiencies of linear narrative in relation to two topics, Vietnam and God. When Skeeter tries to describe Vietnam he tilts his head back 'as if the ceiling is a movie screen' (257/222), allowing a series of visual impressions of the war to flash across his memory. These visual images, however, are not enough to communicate the entire experience. Moving through the sounds and tactile sensations of war, Skeeter recognises that he is still selling his own experience short. Vietnam resists any overall formulation and cannot be parcelled up neatly or sequentially: 'There isn't any net to grab it all in' (258/223). While Skeeter's vision of the war as necessary apocalypse and total sensual experience, in which racial distinctions are dissolved, makes its own ironic comment on McLuhan's sensual and tribal Utopianism, the medium here is McLuhanite. Skeeter's associative, loosely structured monologue communicates fully to Harry who is left wanting to know and to understand in more depth. In religious terms Skeeter sees himself as New Messiah and Black Jesus, in a violent and barbaric second coming. Ironically, however, his Messianic visions are described as descending from the same source as his memories of Vietnam. As Saviour, he says, 'I've come down' (263/227), pointing to the 'movie screen' in the ceiling. While Harry remains somewhat sceptical about this vision of media-induced religious rebirth, Skeeter's multi-media readings and monologues do educate him out of the worst of his racism, and free him to confront both his own exploited status, and his class hatreds (249/215). For all Skeeter's menacing qualities Harry learns enough from him to stand up to this racist neighbours, just as Nelson fights off their children who call him 'Nigger Nellie'.

The contradictory and ambiguous aspects of the characterisation of Skeeter become very evident, however, in two scenes. In the first, Harry's neighbours Showalter and Brumbach, the one in computers, the other an assembly worker in the steel plant, accost Harry, demanding that he eject Skeeter. Up to this point in the novel Harry's neighbours have been very much an offstage presence. Here he is surprised suddenly to notice a mail truck collecting torrents of letters from a mailbox which he always imagined went unused. In the encounter Harry remains cool, noting that the two men's roles, negotiator and muscleman, reflect 'an age of specialisation and collusion' (289/249). The fact that Skeeter, like Brumbach, is a Vietnam veteran cuts no ice at all, however. While Skeeter's presence alerts Harry to the existence of his surrounding neighbours, the message they deliver is a nakedly racist threat, and the eventual outcome hardly suggests the solidarity of the global village.

In the second scene, a trip to the country, Skeeter's bold rhetoric contrasts with his evident dependence on the machine. When the car breaks down, he is fearful, vulnerably conspicuous, his claims that 'blacks are everywhere' merely empty threats. Rescued by an old-fashioned mechanic, Skeeter adopts a slavish Uncle Tom flattery in the taxi home:

Yo' sho' meets a lot ob nice folks hevin' en acci-dent lahk dis, a lot ob naas folks way up no'th heah.   (271/234)

Unlike typographic man, Skeeter has many voices, but is ultimately just as dependent on the roles and resources which he ostensibly decries.

On the individual, emotional level two further episodes emphasise the extent to which Skeeter's rhetoric is also dehumanising and self-serving. In the first Skeeter asks Harry to read to him from Frederick Douglass's account of his life as a slave. Harry complies to protect Nelson from Skeeter's violence: 'if he reads the boy will be safe' (280/241). Beyond the protective 'white island' of the page, Skeeter celebrates sensuality in the 'dark abyss' of the living room. Telling Harry to 'sing it', he strips naked 'to hear it with my pores' (282/243). He proceeds to masturbate, begging Harry to read on: 'Do me one more.' 'It's not the same, right? Doin' it to yourself.' In fairly obvious terms, Skeeter ignores the message here in favour of self-massage, inducing Harry to adopt the role of slave for his own gratification.

The implication that Skeeter is as isolated within his individual reality as the earlier Harry is confirmed in a darker sense in the ensuing scene in which he forces Jill to enact the role of sexually abused black slave-girl. Here the swapping of black and white roles, the oral emphasis, imply exploitation rather than human solidarity. While Skeeter has taught Harry to resist, to fight back, he has also induced Jill to 'shoot', in her case drugs. Jill's steady decline has run in tandem with the developing relationship between Skeeter and Harry. Her cooking has deteriorated into part-burnt, part-frozen offerings and her drawings are now 'linear, arrested' (265/229). The terms in which Harry registers the scene emphasise that Skeeter and the new media enslave as much as their predecessors. Illuminating the couple with a lamp, Harry is reminded, in the first flash, of the printing process, with Jill as white paper, Skeeter as inked plate. The pair appear to him as an interlocked machine. In addition the couple are framed in the blue rectangle of the picture window, a screen. The image of window as screen is developed when Harry changes the screens for storm windows, lovingly cleaning them until 'four flawless transparencies permit outdoors to come indoors. The mirror is two-way' (306/264). Unfortunately this proves all too much of a two-way process. There is a face at the window. The trio's activities are all too open to the viewer at the screen, rumour has broadcast them and they are exposed.

Skeeter's apocalyptic rhetoric and his celebration of multi-media experience culminate in 'the fire this time', the arson of Harry's house, an act of war on the part of his neighbours reasserting their white identity. The fire is announced telephonically by a voice which, initially, may or may not be Skeeter's. The medium here, too cool by half, carries a violent message. Skeeter, who has previously cultivated a 'cool', hip expression, is in reality 'hot', on the run from the police. When the fire explodes, with a sound like an APM in the war, his solidarity crumbles and he reverts to his past basic training. He simply flees, abandoning Jill to the flames. Skeeter has previously celebrated Vietnam as all-inclusive brotherhood and sensual experience. Now Jill is brought from the ruins in a body bag identical to the army's, as badly burned as a napalm victim, unidentifiable as white or black.

Skeeter's comment, 'The war is come home' (334/286), contrasts, however, with the neighbours' reactions. McLuhan's description of Vietnam as the first television war in which the public can be present at the event and participate in it is horribly

parodied here. The onlookers at the fire remain as impassive as if
they were actually watching events on television. Arriving at the
scene Harry is reminded of the crowd watching the earlier
moviemakers in Brewer. Now at the centre of events, Harry still
feels 'peripheral, removed, nostalgic, numb' (319/274). None of
his neighbours come forward 'to sparkle on the bright screen of his
disaster' (330/283). The drama is on the ground, with Nelson,
who struggles with the police but eventually submits, 'relieved to
be at last in the arms of order, of laws and limits' (326/280). Both
the firechief and the watchman guarding the house are
deliberately non-committal, uninvolved. It is not the firechief's
usual beat and he feels no special responsibility. Covering his
notepad with his hand 'as if across the listening mouth of a
telephone receiver' (327/281) he coaches Harry in the right
responses to his question-and-answer series. The pair collude to
obscure the question of responsibility for the fire. Entering the
ruin, in which only the television set remains undamaged, Harry
is told by the watchman that he will not be responsible for Harry's
safety: 'Far as I'm concerned you're not there. See no evil is the
way I do it.' Harry's response, 'That's the way I do it too'
(331/285), underlines his own withdrawal into neutrality. While
he avoids accusing his white neighbours, while he assists Skeeter
in his escape, his last sight of Skeeter, receding into the distance,
framed in his rear-mirror, strikes him as 'oddly right' (337/289).
As the image of rear-mirrorism suggests, Skeeter, the apparent
voice of the future, is travelling backwards, reverting to past
patterns of behaviour (basic training), as caught in the confusions
of his self-image as Jill and Harry.

   The final section of the novel, *Mim*, opens with Harry
typesetting the account of his own tragedy, a message which
cannot be subordinated to its medium. The item remains
unfinished, however, interrupted this time not by Janice but by
the boss who fires him. The *Brewer Vat* is to go offset and be printed
from film in Philadelphia, bypassing hot metal processes entirely.
A few men will be retrained in computers, but the new technology
makes Rabbit redundant. Reduced to dependence on his father's
state pension, Harry returns to his tribe, to be welcomed by Mom
in terms which are heavily ironic. For her, he is worth 'a hundred
doses of L-dopa' (350/300).

   The appearance of Harry's sister, Mim, extends the moral that
McLuhanacy leads to emotional deadness, dependence and state

control. A would-be actress who has become a whore, Mim's large inhuman eyes and abrupt laugh suggest to Harry that a coded tape is being fed through her head, producing 'rapid as electronic images, this alphabet of expressions' (352/302). While Mim's large nose has kept her off the screen, she admits to fulfilling the fantasies of others: 'I take on the audience one at a time' (360/309). When Mim did act in Hollywood it was in Disneyland, dressed in colonial costume, leading tourists around a replica of Mount Vernon. She repeats the performance for her family, her jerky robotic gestures accompanied by a sweetly slow idiotic voice: 'The Fa-ther of our Coun-try was himself nev-er a fa-ther' (362/311). Her own father's affirmative comment, that Disney kept America from Communism during the Depression, reinforces the image of the electronic media as propaganda and control. Mim tells Harry that she has learned to manage and manipulate others, but is herself under gangster control, featuring in her publicity pictures in the role of slave-girl. While the family enjoy the excursion Mim organises to see *Funny Girl*, Mom comments that the film obscures the fact that its heroine was also involved with gangsters. In addition, though ostensibly enjoying sex, Mim has evolved a set of survival rules for living in the new human desert of the West, limiting her erotic performances to three repetitions. Stavros's comment, that in bed Mim's 'thermostat' switched off immediately, leaving him with the sensation of handling rubber, underlines her lack of emotional responsiveness. At this point in the novel Harry is similarly benumbed. His only sexual activity is masturbation, and even then he gains satisfaction only through grotesque fantasies. 'Real people aren't exciting enough' (378/324). He has better luck 'making a movie that he is not in', imagining Mim and Stavros together.

The extent to which the quasi-religious McLuhanite Utopia also fails is explicated in relation to Nelson and Janice. Nelson's reaction to the fire is to blame Harry. Not having been raised to believe in God, 'Blame stops for him in the human world' (325/279). His face 'crazed with some television of remembrance' (350/300), Nelson takes refuge instead in composing a scrapbook on the fire. Its format, which includes news-clippings, doodles, peace-signs, musical notes, Tao crosses and fuzzy Polaroid snaps of the ruin, ironically imitates the form of McLuhan's *The Medium is the Massage*, a similar assemblage of different typographies, headlines, drawings and photographs. It offers Nelson little solace. Janice's decision to leave Stavros, while partly the result of Mim's intervention, also highlights the insufficiency of a life lived entirely in secular and physical terms. When Stavros suffers a near heart attack, Janice recognises that he, too, needs things to be orderly. Importantly, medical technology fails here. Janice is too flustered to find the nitroglycerine tablets, and offers him cold pills instead. Understanding that they are 'beyond chemicals', she feels that she must 'make a miracle' and exorcise the 'devil' within Stavros (386/330). Though Stavros survives, his illness makes the point to her that while 'spirits are insatiable . . . bodies get enough' (388/332). The sensual joy of her relationship is not merely devalued by the example of Mim, but also revealed as insufficient in itself.

Although Janice and Harry are reunited at the close of the novel, the symbolic terms in which their reunion is described leave the final position unresolved. In the course of the novel, different sensory images have been unpacked, revealing the double-edged quality of sensuality, in personal and political terms. At several points Jill and Harry are described as drowning. While Harry survives, surfacing at the point in the novel where the US/USSR ban on underwater weapons is announced, Jill goes under, like Mary Jo Kopechne at Chappaquiddick. Fire imagery includes the warmth of human relations, the 'hot' media, napalm and the burning of the house. The term 'cool' ceases to be affirmative when extended to frozen human beings. Space travelling, floating free may imply liberation and technological triumph, or the dangers of perishing in a cold void. In each case the elemental imagery may be read in two different directions offering messages of opposed types.

At the close of the novel Harry and Janice's communications are similarly ambiguous. Although they succeed in reading each other's silences on the telephone, they are less successful face to face. Harry's attempts to convey by gesture to Janice that she should show the suitcase to the motel clerk are interminably protracted. Contemplating their ruined home, now defaced by contradictory messages, swastikas and peace signs from the same spray can, Harry feels that it all 'adds up no better than the cluster of commercials on TV' (395/338). In the Safe Haven Motel the couple switch off the television and ignore the advertised attractions of the Magic Fingers massage, but their delicate manoeuvrings towards each other are presented in space metaphors. They are 'slowly revolving, afraid of jarring one another away' (396/339), 'slowly adjusting in space', while Harry lets Janice's breasts 'float away, radiant debris' (406/347). The suggestion that Harry 'redocks' here, returning from the void to human contact, is undercut by his comment that he and Janice are made for each other as companion killers. Each flight into freedom has had murderous consequences, for Rebecca in Janice's case, for Jill in Harry's. The last sentence of the novel, 'He. She. Sleeps. O.K.?', while suggesting the over-and-out of a space message, is also uncomfortably close to the robotic voice of Mom. The reunion here is neither a new beginning nor a blessed return, in McLuhanite terms. Any such suggestion is undercut by the contradictory ways in which the fictional message can be read. The novel closes, therefore, on a note of interrogation. While Gutenberg Man has been satirically exposed, while some aspects of the McLuhanite and countercultural synthesis have been treated sympathetically, the new electronic Utopia remains an illusion, and the couple are left in transition. Typographic man may find such an irresolute ending unsatisfying. For the informed reader, however, Updike's refusal to accommodate to the desire for a final 'adding up' or ordered closure, whether linear or cyclic, is entirely appropriate.

Where *Rabbit Redux* focuses upon technological evolution, *Rabbit Is Rich* explores economic change. From its first sentence, 'Running out of gas' (3/7), the novel refers outwards to the rise in oil prices, the American energy crisis of 1979, the declining power of America abroad, challenged by the hostage crisis in Iran, and inwards to the apparently failing physical energy of Harry Angstrom, whose obsessive concern with death expands the frame of reference towards a vision of life as entropic decline. In quite explicit terms the novel questions American systems of values. While Rabbit is rich materially as the prosperous part-owner of the Toyota franchise, a member of the Flying Eagle Country Club, with savings to boot, he is poor in human terms, impoverished in spirit and in his relations to others.

In order to suggest the paucity of Harry's values, Updike draws on three major organising metaphors: anal and libidinal attitudes to money, media fantasies, and information as capital. Readers of *Rabbit Redux* will be familiar with the image of the media as propaganda, purveying a fantasy American dream. In addition, in an extension of McLuhan's thesis, information figures as capital. Given that money is the supreme medium, extending man's grasp from the nearest to more distant staples, it is readily replaced in the next development by the movement of information, so that money merges with informational forms of credit, in this case, particularly, in terms of inside financial information as a capital resource. The third major metaphor treats the fantasies of homo economicus in overtly psychological terms. One dimension of the novel has offended several reviewers, the crudity of the hero's language and the overt sexual and anal detail. Rarely in a novel, with the possible exception of *Tender is the Night* or *Portnoy's Complaint,* have so many major events taken place in bathrooms. The scatological emphasis is relentless from the most common expletive ('shit') to the imagery of waste and waste products, Harry's fascination with male homosexual practices, and his rectal sex with Thelma. An early image establishes connections between energy and waste in both human and economic terms. Stavros is reminiscing about the gas-guzzlers of the past:

> When you took off the filter and looked down through the inlet valve when the thing was idling it looked like a toilet being flushed.   (11/14)

This imagery of waste forms a vital part of Updike's analysis of the power of money in the novel, and necessitates a brief digression into psychoanalytic theory.

The connection between faeces and money has been exhaustively discussed by modern psychoanalytic thinkers, who have developed Freud's original insights in various directions. While it is not within the scope of the present study to engage with these debates in detail, the connection seems an important one.[17] Essentially, the crux of psychoanalytic theories of the anal character of money lies in the idea that faeces are the child's first autonomous product and first material possession, exposing the child also to the power of parents and providing the first opportunity to exercise power over surroundings. By being taught to be clean the child recognises the power of his environment and realises that it is necessary to subordinate self to others. Rewards are obtainable from parents for prompt discharge, and defecation in itself offers auto-erotic pleasure. Alternatively the child may discover that faeces retention provides an opportunity to challenge parents and that such retention may intensify pleasure. In *Three Essays on the Theory of Sexuality* Freud argues that there are four successive stages in the development of sexuality: the polymorphous, oral, anal and genital. Focusing on the 'anal neurotic', the adult who has become arrested in the anal stage, or who has achieved the genital stage so weakly that he later reverts to psychic infantilism, Freud argues that the traits of this character conform to three basic types. Firstly unmodified anal eroticism may express itself openly through coprophilia, homosexuality, or the desire for rectal coitus. Alternatively the instinct may be sublimated, creating an acquisitive, thrifty, miserly character for whom savings replace faeces. Lastly, in reaction, the anal instinct may express itself in an obsessive concern with order and cleanliness, as opposed to dirt, creating an over-conscientious, rigid character type.

Many different types of activity may be understood in terms of Freud's analysis. Getting rid of objects of value may have a libidinous emphasis, as in selling with a profit, pleasurable wastefulness, or gambling. Conversely, hanging on to objects of value, avarice, or collecting, may provide a similar source of pleasure. The small child's delight in moulding clay, making mudpies, or playing in sandpits has also been understood as an expression of the desire to manipulate and handle his 'treasure'. While later theorists (Ferenczi, Abraham, Jones) have contextualised Freud's theories as belonging particularly to bourgeois capitalism with its emphasis on thrift, regular hours and ordered performance, the equation of gold and faeces is also widespread in very different cultures, in folklore (the golden donkey, the goose that lays the golden eggs), in superstitions (bird-droppings on the head are lucky) and in language. Given Updike's linguistic background, he may have noted the high incidence of scatological metaphors for money in colloquial German. English-speaking readers are probably familiar with such expressions as 'to do one's business', 'to make a pile', 'to be tight-assed' (mean) or 'liquid' (in funds), 'to be up shit creek' (in money difficulties) or to possess 'filthy lucre'. Although capitalism may not have created the anal character, it has been argued that it has raised to a high degree of prominence a type which is relatively rare in other social systems. Updike has an illustrious predecessor in calling attention to the connection. In *Our Mutal Friend* Dickens employs the central metaphor of dirtmounds to focus the economic nature of an earlier society.

While Harry Angstrom is not a case study in neuroticism Updike uses the perceived connection between faeces and money in order to illuminate the flaws in Harry's system of values, and the links between money and fantasy. Within this concept even quite minor events in the novel take on a deeper significance. Harry is fascinated, for example, by cars, which have a magical and erotic significance for him. To Mim they are 'shitboxes' (239/221), while to Nelson they are worth acquiring only as 'collectibles'. At the car lot the employees work 'all the shit hours' (264/249), in contrast to Nelson who sees his college degree as 'horse poop' (327/301). Lyle, Slim and the Reverend Campbell are homosexuals. Slim is also a 'stuffer' for the electric light company, putting bills in envelopes – an image which conjoins money, anality and eroticism. Even the erotic activities of the major characters involve sex either in or from the rear (Webb and Cindy, Thelma and Ronnie, Harry and Thelma, Janice and Harry, Nelson and Melanie). In addition, a dominant stylistic feature of the novel, the hero's tendency to catalogue his environment in excessive detail, may be understood less as a documentary approach to Middle America in all its facticity than as an expression of the relentless desire to collect, store up and incorporate information. Importantly, this phenomenon is not limited to Harry. When Pru bombards Nelson with letters packed with information on her pregnancy, Nelson complains that she even tells him 'when she's taken a crap practically' (150/140). It is within this complex framework of associations that certain key plot events and image patterns take on their full resonance.

The opening of the novel foregrounds information as Harry's main capital asset. At the car lot a young rural couple present themselves: 'We chust came in for some information' (14/17). Harry meets the request to excess, bombarding his auditors with mileage figures, technological detail and brand names. The reader is similarly stunned by the description of the Corolla's four-speed synchromesh transmission, fully transistorised ignition system, power assisted front disc brakes and locking gas cap, and the steel-belted radials, quartz crystal clock, and AM/FM stereo of the Celica GT Sport Coupe. The overload of information here is also accompanied by its falsification. When Harry tries to sell the economy model, the Corolla, he quotes

Consumer Reports approvingly, and argues in favour of rapid turnover: 'Who in this day and age keeps a car longer than four years?' (15/18). Seconds later, listing the features of the more expensive Corona, the *Consumer Reports* experts are described as in error in their mileage figures. When the luxury model, the Celica, is the focus, Harry reverses direction again to emphasise its investment value: 'That old Kleenex mentality of trade it in every two years is gone with the wind' (16/19). Harry has an abundance of information here but it is both contradictory and relies on a libidinal emphasis. 'Picking a car is like picking a mate' (16/19) in Harry's view and he puns happily on Japanese currency: 'When trade-in time comes you get your yen back' (16/19). Harry's own 'yen' in the affective meaning of the term is also prominent. The girl who accompanies the prospective purchaser is the daughter of Ruth, Harry's erstwhile lover, and may even be Harry's own child. On the test drive Harry becomes obsessed with this possibility, feeling 'the sudden secret widen within him' (23/25).

In the novel Harry is persistently established as a man who is obsessed with inside commercial knowledge, an avid reader of *Consumer Reports* and a keen listener to Webb Murkett's investment advice. In human terms, however, Harry has the wrong information. While he treasures his erotic or financial secrets, other secrets are withheld from him. He is, for example, the last to discover that Nelson has impregnated Pru, though Janice and her mother swiftly discover this fact. One scene specifically highlights Harry's lack of human information. On a wet evening he is studying *Consumer Reports* while Nelson reads up on the motor industry. As Harry explains the mechanics of car financing in exhaustive detail, he keeps trying to discover what else Nelson has on his mind. Is he sleeping with Melanie? When the subject becomes more delicate, extending to Jill, Harry retreats briskly into accounts of the best four-slice toaster, and fails to see the underlying message in Nelson's cross-questioning on the subject of Stavros's capabilities. When Nelson criticises his father for being 'uptight', Harry listens eagerly, 'thinking this might be information' (119/112), but he lacks the hidden clue which would make everything clear. In each major plot event Harry is similarly the last to discover the right information. He treasures the secret of his Krugerrands and his house, unaware that Janice has already spilled the beans to Nelson. Janice and her mother arrange to fire Stavros and introduce Nelson into the business without Harry being aware of the machinations afoot. Melanie proves a red herring, merely a cover for Pru. Much of the comedy of the novel depends upon Harry's lack of awareness. At Pru's wedding, for example, he notes the gaeity of Campbell and Slim, and assumes that Slim and the organist, fingering each others' shirts, are discussing clothes, failing to see that they are all 'gay' in quite another sense. Harry never suspects that Thelma is attracted to him, though it is crystal clear to Janice, as is his yen for Cindy. Even the wife-swapping in the Caribbean is a surprise to Harry, though the other parties have consulted each other and allocated partners in advance. Finally, Harry never discovers whether Annabelle is his daughter. When he mentions the possibility to Janice, she comments astutely that 'you always want what you don't have instead of what you do' (72/69). Annabelle, unlike the real Nelson, remains a fantasy child. In the final confrontation with Ruth, Harry offers financial support, but is refused in horror, in terms which put his fantasy in its place: 'When I think of you thinking she's your daughter, it's like rubbing her all over with shit' (448/413). This is one secret which money cannot buy. The various revelations of the plot suggest that while Harry hoards his own fantastic secrets, he is blind to other information which is both more important and more real.

It is essential to note that the reader is placed in the same position. Updike makes careful use of proleptic imagery which reveals its true meaning only on a second reading or with hindsight. When Harry sympathises with the young couple, 'I think it's a helluva world we're coming to where a young couple like yourselves can't afford to buy a car or own a home' (23/25), the remark points ahead to anticipate Pru and Nelson's difficulties. When he refuses Nelson a job at the lot because Jake and Rudy are married men 'trying to feed babies on their commissions' (100/95), he little thinks that Nelson is soon to be in the same position. Harry's cosy relation with Stavros has been comfortably accepted, 'When a man fucks your wife, it puts a new value on her' (12/15), but when Webb Murkett does likewise the remark rebounds. While prolepsis often places Harry in an ironic light, the reader is also implicated. Readers may think, for example, that the clipping concerning Skeeter, last seen near Galilee, came from Ruth who lives nearby. When Nelson sees beyond Melanie to 'a more shallow-breasted other' (131/123), the reader has to assume that the absent female is Jill. Pru has not yet been introduced. Hindsight provides an ironic frame, but in the experience of reading, hero and reader advance towards knowledge at the same pace, establishing a strong empathetic relationship which creates a degree of sympathy for Harry. The reader is thus continually invited to consider which information is more valuable, the affective or the economic, the secret fantasy or the human reality.

Since *Rabbit Is Rich* is the third volume of a trilogy, the reader also benefits from hindsight of another type, informed by prior knowledge of Harry's preceding disasters. Harry draws attention to this aspect of events when discussing *Jaws II* with Cindy: 'D'you ever get the feeling everything these days is sequels? Like people are running out of ideas' (403/371). In plot terms, Nelson's impregnation of Pru, his absorption into the family business and his later flight from domestic responsibilities, suggest that the past conditions the present and that its horrors are merely repeated by the second generation. Nelson clearly mimics the earlier Harry's racism, and after an initial flirtation with vegetarian, mystical Melanie, a similar figure to Jill, marries a woman who is in appearance strongly reminiscent of Mom Angstrom. In addition a succession of media images offer two alternative interpretive frames for the family events of the novel, as pleasant repetition or as reenacted horrors. Harry exists in a world dominated by media fantasies. At the country club his crowd act loudly and boisterously, modelling their behaviour on TV beer commercials. The bronzed Murketts hug each other, 'framed as if for an ad' (172/160) against the background of Mount Pemaquid. In his car Harry listens to pop music, particularly the John Travolta theme song, which recalls the dominant feeling of the preceding summer, with 'every twat under fifteen wanting to be humped by a former Sweathog in the back seat of a car parked in Brooklyn' (33/35). The imagery suggests that in economic terms corporate capital reproduces itself by controlling desire to create new consumer wants and a mass market. Harry's own Toyota franchise depends upon a similar creation of mass fantasy in its advertising campaign ('Oh what a feeling!').

Within this general framework two specific media-genres are counterpointed. The women of the novel revel in television soap opera. Harry's antagonistic discussions of past horrors, with Nelson, are repeatedly interrupted by Janice and her mother, wiping their eyes from an episode of *The Waltons*, *The Jeffersons* or

All in the Family. At several points an ironic counterpoint is established between screen image and Angstrom family. When, for example, Nelson returns to demand money and a job, with attendant complications, Mrs Springer retreats into a re-run episode of *All in the Family* in which a character's old girlfriend also asks for money. As Nelson and Harry clash over the job at the lot, Janice interrupts, laughing at herself for being so carried away by *The Waltons*, when 'It was in *People* how all the actors couldn't stand each other' (120/113). In each case the women are watching re-runs, and in each case the repeated screen image of American Happy Families is undercut by the real conflicts in the Angstrom home. Harry dislikes the TV series, Nelson is equally irritated as Pru succumbs increasingly to pregnancy and the lure of afternoon soaps. Nelson does enjoy one episode of the series *Charlie's Angels*, laughing empathetically as huge automobilies collide in slow motion. When, however, Nelson acts out the fantasy, demolishing the convertibles, the climax is registered not in the slow motion of fantasy, but as comically fast. Far from enjoying a fantasy triumph, Nelson sobs in Harry's arms, while Harry repeats the slogan, 'Oh what a feeling' (170/158). The episode undercuts the advertisement much as the preceding slogan 'You asked for it we got it' suggested ironically that, in the oil crisis, America got what it asked for in a less affirmative sense. Although Harry has been scornful of the fantasy family image, hating to see the Pittsburgh football team win because their image depends upon 'all that Family crap' (269/248), he has been too swift to discount the force of real human emotion, as opposed to commercial mass fantasy. As he comments, 'Funny about feelings. They seem to come and go in a flash and yet outlast metal' (163/153).

In opposition to the female soap opera an alternative image of the family as horror obsesses the men. At Nelson's wedding, Harry notes the Reverend Campbell emerging from the vestry as if 'from a secret door like in a horror movie' (242/224). For Harry the wedding is selling Nelson down the river. He has previously imagined Pru's father as a 'sorehead who wants to strangle his daughter and put her in the potato bin' (230/213), and his memories of rural horror stories, incest and murder, as related in the *Brewer Vat*, undercut the cosy image of the rural past now on show to tourists at the Albrecht Stamm Homestead in Brewer. Nelson's image of the family is vividly suggested by his fascination with the *Amityville Horror* film, in which an ordinary home is occupied by the devil. Nelson repeatedly describes his past as a horror story, and was initially attracted to Pru by her 'horror stories of her own growing up' (315/291), beatings, rages and tangled family tensions. Nelson's exaggerated image of his father coincides with a remembered picture of an ogre in a children's book, with blubbery lips and hairy face: 'That's how he sees Dad these days' (361/333). When Nelson repeats his griefs to Pru, however, she dismisses them as no worse than other people's experiences. As they talk Nelson observes a framed print of a goateed farmer in his room. In the past the print had seemed 'a leering devil' (318/293), but is now 'merely foolish, sentimental'. For all their overt hostility the two men are intimately connected through their shared fantasies, and both have to learn to see the reality instead.

At Slim's party fantasy and horrors merge, undercutting the exaggerated image. Nelson's hostility to pregnant Pru had previously led him into reverie about freefall parachuting in *Moonraker*. At the party the couple argue in a room filled with grotesque pornographic images of women and boys. Mesmerised by these obscene pictures, moving 'from one horror to another' (335/309), Nelson lets Pru slip away from him, and takes refuge in the bathroom, fascinated by an album of Nazi pornography. Images of horror precede the actual accident, when Pru slips from Nelson's grasp and freefalls down the stairs. In the event, disaster is averted. Pru does not lose the baby, but merely breaks an arm. In the action of the novel melodramatic horrors repeatedly threaten but fail to materialise. There is no death (despite the frailty of Stavros and Thelma), no financial ruin, and such accidents as do occur are mostly minor automobile scrapes. Nelson does not commit incest with his sister, though the possibility hovers, and even the wife-swapping culminates in cosy chat about children. Neither of the mass fantasies is therefore confirmed. The careful alternation between the two media frames, soaps and horrors, keeps the reader from assessing the events of the novel in terms of mass fantasy, undercutting the image of American Happy Families, while refusing to cater for the opposite suggestion of America as horror. In the final pages of the novel Harry watches the Superbowl on television, particularly the half-time show with its orchestrated American propaganda. 'Sentimental Journey' is sung, followed by dancers flashing tinfoil solar panels, singing 'Energy is people'. Harry turns away from the television,

however, to his granddaughter who is described in exactly the
same terms as Rebecca in *Rabbit, Run,* 'She knows she's good'
(467/429). This is a real child, neither the daughter of fantasy nor
a remembered horror from the past. Where the Superbowl
dancers celebrate naive patriotism, Harry's final comment refers
less affirmatively to the Iranian hostages: 'Fortune's hostage,
heart's desire, a granddaughter. His. Another nail in his coffin.
His' (467/429). The new child reminds Harry of the past, of failing
energy, of death and yet also of fulfilled desire. In a sense, Harry
has given hostages to fortune, his family, and emerges from
fantasy only at the end of the novel when he realises their true
value. While the novel points towards a humanist message in
which human beings are more important than money, it is not
itself a sentimental journey. Any such reading is checked by the
continual undercutting of soap opera and mass media imagery.

Harry takes some time, none the less, to appreciate the real
bases of his fortune. Initially his attitude to his family appears
to be entirely conditioned by his economic position. In particular
his sexual life has been affected by his new wealth. Although he is
rich because of Janice's inheritance, having money has made him
feel 'satisfied all over' (49/49) leading to an energy crisis all his
own. Of recent years his sexual interest has begun 'to wobble,
and by now there is a real crisis of confidence' (49/49). Nelson's
return wakes Harry up once more. He tells Janice that 'It's great
to have an enemy. Sharpens your senses' (125/117). Where Harry
is miserly, Nelson is wasteful, a continual drain on his father's
resources, landing him with car repair bills, an expensive wedding
and Pru's hospital charges. In the course of the novel Harry
evolves from anal hoarder to pleasurable spender, an evolution
assisted by Nelson who tells him that 'Money is shit' (169/157).

Two key scenes establish the libidinal associations which
money has for Harry. In the first, money and sex are intimately
conjoined. Acting on Webb's inside information on the money
market, Harry takes his savings from the bank and converts them
into Kruggerands at a shop in Brewer. The terms of the
description here are explicitly anal. 'Fiscal Alternatives' is
situated opposite a shop which sells 'dirty magazines for queers'
(210/195) and looks itself as if it might be 'peddling smut'. The
coins come in plastic containers with round lids which suggest
tiny toilet seats: 'Bits of what seemed toilet paper were stuffed into
the hole of this lid to make the fit tight' (211/195). Hiding the coins

away Harry moves through two memories, one of surprising
Nelson, massively phallic in the shower, the other of catching his
father, vulnerably naked: 'such white buttocks, limp and hairless,
mute and helpless flesh that squeezed out shit once a day'
(212/197). As the two memories suggest, Harry, endowed with his
gold, feels a renewed sexual power, distancing himself from the
image of the aging father. Nelson, who has just spent an evening
with the Reverend Campbell, is now under threat. Harry enjoys
his son's irreverent comment on the homosexual pastor's
continual description of the Church as the Bride of Christ: 'What
does he do, fuck the church up the ass?' (213/197). The repeated
anal references precede the scene, reminiscent of a similar
luxuriation in gold in Norris's *McTeague*, in which Janice and
Harry make love amidst the Krugerrands. The gold here appears
to recreate Harry's sense of sexual identity and to recharge his
batteries. Imitating funerary rites (pennies for the ferryman)
Harry positions two coins on his eyelids, and then removes them,
'a dead man reborn' (216/201), tumescent amid scattered gold.
The scene also dramatises the extent to which Janice is the
foundation of Harry's fortune. Balancing coins all over her, he
cautions her to lie still: 'If she laughs and her belly moves the
whole construction will collapse' (218/202). Harry has previously
enjoyed Janice's 'new sense of herself as a prize' (188/175),
commenting that there is 'nothing like fucking money'. When he is
summoned home by Janice to meet Pru her guarded tones make
him think that she is being held hostage. Nelson, who is in a sense
holding Harry to ransom, is also associated with the Iranian
hostages: 'Khomeini and Carter both trapped by a pack of kids
who need a shave and don't know shit' (354/327). Harry's private
fantasy assertion of his sexual power is thus imagistically
connected with political and economic realities. While the
couple's love-making is ecstatic, the description, in financial
terminology, is highly ironic. Coins spill between Janice's legs as
Harry's 'interest compounds' until, after the final 'payoff', the
spent hero engages in a comically panic-stricken hunt for a lost
coin.

When Harry later converts his hoarded gold into silver, darker
suggestions undercut the preceding pleasurable enactment of his
deepest fantasies. The anal emphasis recurs. Janice asks, 'How
liquid is this silver?' and the coins are brought in by Nelson's
homosexual friend Lyle. Sorting the coins, Janice titters, and

Harry understands why: 'playing in the mud' (368/339). Unlike
the Krugerrands, however, the silver is less magically attractive,
consisting of old coins which have already been sifted for collector
value. They are also extremely heavy, so that handling them is less
a pleasure than a chore. Perversity and grotesqueness pervade the
scene. Lyle squints at Harry as if the latter had bought 'not only
the massage but the black-leather-and-whip trick too' (368/339).
Sweating and struggling to the bank, Janice figures as a gross
image of maternity, cradling her sack as if it were a baby, in an
ironic image of reproductive capitalism in action. In the bank the
Angstroms attempt to stuff their safe deposit box, but finally have
to abandon their efforts, apologising to the teller for having
'loaded it up with so much crap' (374/345). Where the gold
appeared magically erotic, the silver is described in terms which
associate it with dirt and death. Although Harry feels a furtive
rush of desire for Janice in the bank vault he speedily realises that
it is 'Not a good place to fuck'. The safety deposit box is described
as sliding into the wall like a coffin in a vault. As they leave the
bank Harry feels only loss:

> His silver is scattered. . . . It's all dirt anyway. He glimpses the
> truth that to be rich is to be robbed, to be rich is to be
> poor.   (375/346)

In the movement between the two scenes Updike conveys Harry's
dawning realisation that money is not magical treasure, life-
giving in erotic terms, and that death undercuts the physical and
materialist fantasy in which he lives. Material riches rob him of
human emotions and render him poor in spiritual and
psychological terms.

It is important to note that Harry's fantasies are not purely the
product of individual neurosis but are representative, a point
indicated in the evening spent at the Murketts', which generalises
his position. Just as Webb Murkett has access to financial inside
information, his job as a contractor provides him with superior
plumbing fixtures. Harry is enchanted by the guest bathroom
with its Popeye toilet paper, monogrammed towels and furry seat
cover. The bathroom is so sparklingly clean that it appears to be
unused. Its furnishings, catalogued over some two pages,
emphasise an obsessional concern with the display of order and
cleanliness. When, however, Harry opens the medicine cabinet its

contents hints at darker secrets. The ostensibly relaxed Murketts
have a battery of medicaments to hand, including Maalox for
stomach ulcers and Preparation H for haemorrhoids. Harry's
comment suggests his growing awareness of the connection
between money and anality:

> Carter of course has haemorrhoids, that grim over-motivated
> type who wants to do everything on schedule ready or not,
> pushing, pushing. (285/263)

Back in the living-room, entranced once more by the ostentatious
Murketts as living embodiments of the American dream, Harry's
thoughts turn libidinous. Are the pellets for erotic use?
'Everybody loves an ass. Those wax bullets in the yellow box –
could they have been for Cindy? Sore there from, but would
Webb?' (286/264). In the background money and secrets recur.
Murketts, Angstroms and Harrisons form the inner circle of the
party, while the Fosnachts are outsiders. Ronnie Harrison, who
depends for his living as an insurance agent on the threat of death,
spends part of the evening bombarding Ollie Fosnacht with
financial information, humiliating him just 'to see how much
garbage he could eat' (295/275). Peggy, unaware that Cindy is a
Catholic, commits a social gaffe in her attack on the Pope, the
result of not having the information on Cindy which the others
share.

When Peggy blocks the guest toilet, mopping up her tears with
Kleenex, Harry goes upstairs to use the domestic facilities. Money
and Cindy are on his mind in almost equal proportions. Urinating
he fills the bowl with gold. 'His bubbles multiply like coins'
(302/278), as he thinks of his savings. Upstairs Harry discovers
Polaroid photographs of Webb and Cindy having sex. At the
party the Murketts have been embracing 'like a loving pair
advertising vacations abroad' (298/275), posing as the ideal
couple of fantasy. In the late afternoon light of the photos the
couple again appear 'golden' (307/283). Closer observation,
however, reveals the flaws in the image. Although this section of
the novel was published as an excerpt in *Playboy*, the images are
actually designed to undercut the mass libidinal fantasy. Posing
as if for a centrefold, Cindy is described as a grotesque, truncated
object. Because of the camera angle her face is out of focus beyond
her drooping breasts, her chin is doubled, and her feet, in the

deficient perspective, look enormous. A second snap catches only her buttocks and their Cyclopean 'eye'. Squinting, Harry deciphers a fuzzy background as Webb's chest, a bulge as Cindy's face, Webb's pot-belly, feeble erection and 'shit-eating expression', but the overall effect left by the photographs is distinctly unenticing. Webb and Cindy are considerably less 'golden' than they would like to appear, and while Harry is excited he is also repelled by the overt 'dirtiness' of the images. In response Harry reverts to his own secrets: 'He tries to discipline what he has seen with his other secrets. His daughter. His gold. His son' (308/284). Only the thought of Nelson is sufficient to bring him back to earth.

Back again at the party Harry spots the two remaining Polaroids. Importantly Webb has used only two exposures to picture his children. Earlier Harry had noted that Webb's display of colour photos had captured the children of his previous marriages but had been edited to exclude the wives, represented only by an amputated hand or arm in the background. Webb had previously described to Harry how he drove his adult children away, breaking off all contact. In the two Polaroids the son stands 'sadly' on the patio, the daughter squints foolishly, menaced by her father's large shadow. On one level the scene draws a parallel between Webb and Harry, each neglecting their real children to focus upon fantasy images, and abandoning mature wives in favour of child-women who are purely the objects of male desire. Mass fantasy has clearly affected Webb's emotional life to its detriment. Though Harry is still in transition at this stage of the novel, the episode suggests that human responsibilities (here, Nelson) form a necessary discipline, and that human affections and emotions are more complex than the one-dimensional centrefold image allows. Later, emerging from fantasy, Harry finds a stack of old pornographic magazines in his new house. Though he flicks through the centrefolds to reveal the slow widening of the models' legs, until full pubic display is permitted, he remains quite unmoved. The sexual secret is not everything. The girls' genitals merely 'act as a barrier to some secret beyond' (458/421). In the Caribbean vacation this beyond figures prominently as the last of Harry's fantasies is definitively exploded.

At the Murketts' Harry had announced, 'I want to go to the Caribbean. But first I want to go to the bathroom. Bathroom,

home, Caribbean in that order' (301/278). Later events reverse
the sequence as Harry travels to the Caribbean, indulges in
bathroom activities with Thelma, and returns home. On one level
the vacation is part of his evolution from saver to spender,
following as it does upon the purchase of the house which wipes
out his savings. Each of Harry's previous holidays reflected his
economic position, from his childhood trips to the shore, the
outings of the poor, to his holidays in the Poconos, dependent on
Janice's parents. The vacation in the islands is the ultimate
fantasy, enjoyed by rich Americans in a protected enclave, fenced
off from the background of Caribbean poverty.

In the plane, rising above the material world below, Harry has
a fleeting religious intimation: 'God, having shrunk in Harry's
middle years . . . is suddenly great again' (390/359). Beneath the
new constellations of the Caribbean, however, Harry's spending
takes on a less spiritual guise. When Janice worries about the size
of their final bill Harry is sanguine.' The expense in his mind is
party of a worthy campaign, to sleep with Cindy' (396/364).
Harry's pleasurable wastefulness almost produces its desired
libidinal reward. After he loses $300 in the Casino, Cindy
approaches him beside the sea, and it seems as if their moment has
come. The pair are immediately interrupted by the news that
Ronnie Harrison is 'burning up the crap table inside' (400/368).
Though Ronnie ends up only a few dollars ahead, it is in fact he
who gains Cindy, described here as Webb's 'treasure to barter'.
The wife-swapping deliberately organises human sexuality in
terms of exchange values. Webb cautions that it must not be
repeated, and must be purely sexual, non-romantic (407/375).
While Ronnie, star of the crap table, gains Cindy, Janice chooses
Webb, entranced by his commercial 'bullshit'.

The faecal suggestions in the two images are developed in
Harry's anal intercourse with Thelma. On one level the scene is
highly ironic. Harry is bitterly disappointed in his allocated
partner. In the event, though, the night with Thelma proves oddly
liberating. Initially Harry's desire is merely to get through the
evening, to save his energies for Cindy on the following night. In
the Harrisons' bathroom the thrifty emphasis recurs. Harry
contemplates the conspicuous consumption evident in their
toiletries, from the pressurised ozone-eating shaving cream, to the
monster toothpaste and new razor: 'Harry can't see the point, it's
just more waste' (411/379). When Thelma appears, however, clad

in cocoa bra and black panties, which she discards into a 'dirty pile' of laundry, Harry finds her more enticing than he had imagined, and eagerly accepts her sexual offer. But when this event occurs, the fantasy is demystified. Penetrating Thelma, Harry feels, 'There is no sensation: a void, a pure black box, a casket of perfect nothingness' (417/384). The terms refer back to the safe deposit box, and to funerary caskets, rather than to treasure trove. When Harry finally enacts the fantasy underlying his behaviour, he sees through it to the emptiness at its centre. Thelma's impending death from lupus also has a symbolic resonance. Lupus, a tubercular skin condition, is a consuming disease, hence its name, and connects to other images of greedy consumption in the novel. At home with death, Thelma reawakens Harry's 'sense of miracle at being himself' (419/386). Their long conversation, centred on their children, emphasises that Harry has not reverted to psychic infantilism, but has conquered it, reassuming his role as a father. Thelma points out that to young girls like Cindy he is 'just an empty heap of years and money' (420/386), whereas to her he is both real and unique. When, the next morning, Harry discovers that he must return home, Nelson having gone missing, his reaction is mixed. Though irritated at missing Cindy, he also feels that in a way 'this is a relief' (426/392). Listening to Janice's tale of woe, he is infuriated by Webb's knowing comments, hating 'people who seem to know; they would keep us blind to the fact that there is nothing to know. We are each of us filled with a perfect blackness' (425/391). Sexual and commercial secrets are exploded together, as false knowledge, companion voids. Beneath the plane the riches of America are now distanced and irrelevant. Harry had previously imagined the American South as a land of wealth, butlers, and above all attractive women. Now, 'the possibility of such women is falling from him' and he prays silently and turns to Janice. The night with Thelma is assessed as 'in texture no different from the dream. Only Janice is real' (427/393). Weeping, exchanging expressions of love, the two clasp hands, floating above the revealed void.

Events do not of course conclude on such an unambiguous, potentially 'soapy' note. Harry returns to both a new beginning and new responsibilities. Though Nelson is no longer perceived as a threat, though Mrs Springer appears to have shrunk in size, Thelma is not so easily shaken off. At the close of the novel she sends Harry a clipping, an account of a Baltimore physician who killed a goose on a golf course. This story is told several times in the novel. When Harry first hears it on the radio, he understands it as involving the mercy-killing of an injured bird, rather than 'murder most foul' and re-tells the joke at the club. Thelma later uncovers a clipping of the story in a syndicated column, in which a Washington doctor is described as beating the goose to death as he was about to sink his putt – a very different version. When Harry sees geese on Ruth's pond he wonders if the doctor killed the bird because of the 'little green turds' which geese leave on the fairway. In the final version the doctor has been fined $500 and is described as having 'cooked his own goose' (454/418). The evolution of the story accompanies Harry's own evolution, alternatively emphasising false information, anality and financial loss in a series of different media versions which recast the event as joke or horror. Potentially the story suggests that in sleeping with Thelma, Harry has cooked his particular golden goose, Janice. Thelma is in love with Harry and is unlikely to respect the terms of the exchange. Indeed, the Angstroms' first day in their new home is soured by the preceding night's party with the gang. None the less when Janice voices her unease, Harry defuses the threat, hugging her to him and reassuring her that the Harrisons are as ordinary as they are, and that he will never run again. Reflecting, Harry remembers a Princeton Professor's theory that 'in ancient times the gods spoke to people directly through the left or was it the right half of their brains' (462/424), a system which later broke down. The reference (to Julian Jaynes, *The Origins of Consciousness in the Breakdown of the Bicameral Mind*, 1976) suggests that Harry has begun to perceive, for all his materialism, the existence of a possible human relationship to a greatery mystery.

Though Updike is too realistic to convert Harry wholesale at the end of the novel, the image of Harry's new house also suggests a compromise between saving and spending, between past materialism and a dawning realisation of other possibilities. Updike draws here upon Thoreau, whose *Walden*, particularly the 'Economy' chapter, describes the author's symbolic house-hunting and his withdrawal from a materialist world to a simplified existence at Walden Pond. Throughout *Rabbit Is Rich* reference is made to Thoreau, and to images of rural simplicity (the Poconos vacation, the woodchuck which Nelson swerves to avoid, Melanie's horror of animal food). While the poverty of Ruth's rural home, with its rusting buses, fallen fruit, and general atmosphere of decay, undercuts any pastoral moral, Rabbit finally occupies a small house, which is curtainless and stripped to its essentials, like Thoreau's, and looks out on a small ornamental pond and squirrels. The conclusion of the novel suggests, if tentatively, that Harry has transcended the worst of materialism, to perceive with Thoreau that the only standard of value lies in vital human experience, as opposed to the complexities of civilisation which stand in the way of significant life. Though the things of the world have not been cast off, they have been reassessed and placed in relation to a potentially spiritual if muted conclusion.

4

The Aesthetic Sphere: *The Centaur, Of the Farm, Marry Me* and *A Month of Sundays*

While Updike's major achievements are essentially realistic novels, in a mimetic mode which emphasises specificity of representation in a social context, a powerful undercurrent also runs through his work, in which more fantastic, self-conscious and metafictional novels centre upon artistic questions. Two collections of short stories (*Bech: A Book* and *Bech is Back*) take the writer as their protagonist, while the plastic arts figure prominently in Updike's poetry and such short stories as 'Museums and Women', 'Still Life' and 'Packed Dirt' among others. Four novels are particularly interesting in this connection: *The Centaur, Of the Farm, A Month of Sundays* and above all, *Marry Me*, which merits an extended discussion. Each features an artist manqué as protagonist (respectively, an expressionist painter, a would-be poet turned ad-man, a writer of sermons, a failed cartoonist). Each foregrounds the nature of illusion or myth, most noticeably the Greek mythology of *The Centaur* and the family myth of *Of the Farm*, and each is highly self-conscious in form, moving away from the realist novel towards other genres: elegy (*The Centaur*), novella (*Of the Farm*), diary (*A Month of Sundays*) and romance (*Marry Me*). Individually each novel may be described as a *Künstlerroman* or aesthetic allegory. Taken as a group they illuminate the evolution of Updike's aesthetic.

Any discussion of this aesthetic, however, necessitates some careful definition of terms, particularly in relation to the influence of Søren Kierkegaard, the Danish existential philosopher. In interview Updike has said that he fell in love with Kierkegaard in his twenties, finding his idea of existence as preceding essence intensely liberating in personal terms:

> it seemed to give me a handle on my own life. As a young person I felt that thinking of myself as being suspended quite pointlessly in an immense void of indifferent stars and mathematically operating atoms made it difficult to justify action. To act because, if you don't, you'll get hungry – to act simply because of animal reaction to stimuli – was not to act in a way that gave shape to life. Justification was not there and it was a problem to me. I read the existentialists seeking a handle for something that had been hard to grasp, and thinking about life in this way enabled me to become involved in life as an average, enterprising, and organised person.[18]

Inevitably Kierkegaard has also had a perceptible influence on Updike as a practising artist.

Kierkegaard uses the term 'aesthetic' in two senses, firstly in its usual meaning, to refer to art and artistic theory, secondly to denote the 'aesthetic sphere of existence'.[19] For Kierkegaard, existence belongs at any given point to one of three spheres, the aesthetic, the ethical and the religious. In the aesthetic sphere the individual lives to enjoy life; the aesthetic life is the life of immediacy. Aesthetic existence is not just hedonism, however. Rather, its essence is that life is divorced from moral will and completely determined by external events. To live aesthetically is to live without choosing, in an immediate continuity of nature and feeling, before any moral distinctions are attempted. The aesthetic level therefore leaves the meaning of life at the mercy of fate or fortune. The succeeding sphere, the ethical, involves not so much a 'good life' as a life governed by the principle of voluntary decisions. The distinguishing criterion between the aesthetic and the ethical is the 'baptism of the will'. What is important here is not the reality of the things chosen, so much as the act of choice itself. The third sphere, the religious, involves the acceptance of suffering as the principle of life. Where the desire for momentary pleasure governs the aesthetic, that of eternal happiness governs the religious. Whereas the individual in the aesthetic sphere is dependent on external factors, equating suffering with misfortune, and thus either keeping the self at a distance from existence, or being in existence as a state of illusion, the existential individual dedicates himself to the task of existing and of penetrating illusions. It is important to note here that Kierkegaard's concept of existential action relates not merely to action in the external world, but to inwardness, that is, to attempts to transform the individual's own inner existence. Suffering is the highest action of inwardness and is therefore essential to life, *not* accidental as the individual in the aesthetic sphere maintains. 'Existence' may thus be defined as that process of transition through free decisions and actions by means of which the child becomes qualitatively different.

In Kierkegaard's view the only reality that can be known is the internal or existential; the reality which we seize is our own person in its flow through time. For Kierkegaard, truth is subjectivity. To paraphrase Theodor Haecker, rather than going from the things over the person to the things, Kierkegaard wants to go from the person over the things to the person. He begins his enquiry, not from the world given in sense impressions, but from the existing ego of the individual being. He then views the world from this standpoint. Truth is therefore understood as the relation of the subject (not the thinking subject, but the subjective individual) to reality. This subjectivity should be distinguished from subjectivism (the idea that the only reality we can know is our own individual consciousness). Kierkegaard never argues that the objective world is an illusion of the senses. For him objectivity meant the method of conceiving reality as an object of thought, apart from the observer's actual subjective being as an existing ego. In his argument we partake of reality not as thinkers but as living subjects. Where the objective thinker sits on the balcony of life, viewing it from without, the subjective is down in the road, a part of life. Truth is therefore not a doctrine to which we relate ourselves intellectually; it is existence, our individual subjective relation to reality. As a result, Kierkegaard's own theory of art rejects the preeminence of thought in engagement with reality, granting art a special value. The artistic process becomes the process of communication of subjectivity. In Kierkegaard's perception, the paradoxical tensions at the heart of existence (that man is an infinite spirit and an isolated consciousness, that in existence the timeless and the temporal meet) lend themselves only to artistic and indirect communication. Thus, Kierkegaard selects, as an example, the problem of death, arguing that because of its personal character, it can never be dealt with adequately in philosophy, or, as an ultimate event, philosophically understood. The poetic rendering of death in lyrics is therefore more effective than what philosophers may have said. Where Idealist philosophers (e.g. Hegel) transform aesthetics into metaphysics. arguing that art manifests the infinite in the finite, or presents an ideal or spiritual reality, Kierkegaard argues that art is a process of communication. It does not reconcile us with reality, nor can it serve as a revelation. Kierkegaard's aesthetic theory is therefore less metaphysical than empirical, and it thus perceives language as the most valuable of media, in that, in its concreteness, it is more empowered to communicate than the more 'abstract' media.

The relation between the aesthetic and the religious constitutes the major focus of *The Centaur*. From his studio, Peter Caldwell, in his own description a 'second-rate abstract expressionist' (102/ 95), ponders and recreates his family history. As successor to a preacher-grandfather and teacher-father, Peter detects a reversal of the Kierkegaardian scale of aesthetic, ethical and religious. 'Priest, teacher, artist: the classic degeneration' (269/243). It is important to note, however, that this realisation comes to the mature Peter only at the close of his story, which records the events of three days of his adolescence, reinterpreting and reassessing his attitudes to art, and to his father George. Alice and Kenneth Hamilton have argued persuasively that *The Centaur* is dominated by George Caldwell's struggle against Kierkegaard's 'sickness unto death', despair. In the course of the story, George, who exists in the ethical sphere, learns to accept the discipline of suffering and sacrifice, and is reconciled to death. The starting point for the novel is George's science lesson, in which the presentation of creation in terms of an immense void of 'indifferent stars and mathematically operating atoms' (to quote Updike's previous statement) incites his class to riot and George himself to violent, unjustified action. George turns away disillusioned, 'his very blood loathed the story he had told' (46/45).

Updike's novel, however, is also the story of Peter, the artist, and his developing awareness that his understanding of his art is deficient. In an essay on 'The Artist and His Audience' (*New York Review of Books*, 18 July 1985, 14–18) Updike has commented upon art in terms which broadly suggest agreement with Kierkegaard's distate for the abstract media:

The will towards concreteness, the fervor to do justice to the real, compels style and form into being. No style or form exists in the abstract.

As an adolescent, Peter had admired that least abstract of painters, Vermeer. What attracts him to Vermeer, however, is less the specificity of the image than its apparent immutability, transcending time and change. For Peter, art offers 'the potential fixing of a few passing seconds' (62/59). As a result he converts aesthetics into metaphysics. Vermeer's *A Young Woman with a Water Jug* becomes 'the Holy Ghost' (85/80) of his adolescence, and he imagines a future career painting 'pictures heavenly and cool', works of 'featureless radiance' (78/74). Peter's transcendental aesthetic becomes a substitute for engaging with existence. In plain terms he is a terrible snob, disdaining his rural surroundings and companions. After one encounter with the neighbouring children, whom he describes as savages, remote from his own highly civilised aspirations, he plunges back with relief into his book of Vermeer reproductions. Significantly Peter only knows the Vermeers in an ideal form. He is never able to see the paintings themselves, with their 'tracery of the cracks whereby time had inserted itself' (85/80). Updike has noted that his own style of writing tends to be pictorial, both in the desire for visual precision, and in his conception of his novels as objects in space. 'I do not recommend this approach. . . . Storytelling, for all its powers of depiction, shares with music the medium of time, and perhaps its genius, its most central transformation, has to do with time, with rhythm and echo and the sense of time not frozen as in a painting, but channelled and harnessed as in a symphony' (*Picked-Up Pieces*, pp. 35–6). In contrast, the youthful Peter demonstrates a royal scorn for narrative (specifically his father's tendency to tell his story to all and sundry) and sees everything in highly pictorial terms: a frozen landscape as a Dürer (75/71), an eroded lawn as green paint rubbed with sandpaper (52/50), his girl Penny as 'a fresh patch of paint' (51/50) in his life. Peter uses art as an escape route from the ugly realities of the present, into the timeless. He is particularly unwilling to confront the realities of Nature and the body. When a homosexual hitches a lift with his father he is disgusted:

> That my existence at one extremity should be tangent to Vermeer and at the other to the hitchhiker seemed an unendurable strain. (83/78)

Peter's ambivalence to the body is also expressed in his attitude to his psoriasis, a flaking skin condition which fills him with self-loathing, and which he therefore transforms into a 'rhythmic curse' (53/51) imposed by God. Peter's description of his belly, dotted with scabs 'as if pecked by a great bird' (52/51), suggests that he understands his psoriasis as a claim to, and a consequence of his special status as an artist. In the mythological structure of the novel Peter figures as Prometheus, who stole fire from the gods as a gift to man, and thus became the founder of all the arts. Zeus punished his transgression by chaining Prometheus to a rock, where his entrails were daily pecked out by an eagle. When Peter dons a red shirt, he sees it as a gift to his classmates on a wintry day, 'a giant spark, a two-pocketed emblem of heat' (55/53). The identification of Peter with Prometheus correlates with Peter's arrogant assumption that the creative artist can challenge the gods to become a benefactor to lesser mortals, his suffering not a normal part of existence, but a mark of privileged status.

An alternative understanding of aesthetics is indicated when Peter collects his father from a visit to Doc Appleton, the figure in the novel who represents Apollo, god of healing, light and poetry. In the doctor's vestibule Peter notices a small print, 'frightful to look at, of some classical scene of violence' (125/115). For Peter the print is a horror, so depressing that he can hardly bring himself to focus upon it: 'my impression was vaguely of a flogging' (125/115). In the mythological index to the novel Updike identifies the print as portraying the flaying of Marsyas, a favourite subject for painters, treated by Raphael, Tintoretto, Titian, Rubens and Perugino, among others. In the myth Marsyas challenged Apollo to a musical contest, lost and was subsequently skinned alive. As Edgar Wind has demonstrated (*Pagan Mysteries in the Renaissance*, Faber, 1958) Marsyas was a follower of Dionysos, and his flute the Bacchic instrument for arousing the dark passions, whereas Apollo, on his divine lyre, tuned the harmonies of the spheres. In Wind's authoritative explication, the flaying represents a tragic ordeal of purification, by which the ugliness of the outer man is thrown off, and a beautiful inner self revealed. Thus, to obtain the laurel of Apollo, the artist must first pass through the agony and suffering of Marsyas. Nietzsche's consideration of the Apollonian and Dionysian aesthetics (in *The Birth of Tragedy*) is also suggestive here. For Nietzsche the Dionysian perspective involves acknowledging without reserve both guilt and suffering, and all that is strange and questionable in human life. In his view, the Greeks, keenly aware of the horrors of existence, placed before them the shining fantasy of their Olympian gods, in order to be able to live at all. Where Dionysian art makes us confront dark realities, Apollonian art emphasises light and clarity, celebrating all those illusions which make life worth living, and cover its dissonance with a veil of beauty. According to Nietzsche, it is the conjunction of the two aesthetics which gives birth to the supreme artistic realisation, Greek tragedy. The flaying of Marsyas also suggests a parallel with Peter, 'flayed' by psoriasis. Significantly Doc Appleton also has psoriasis. Potentially therefore Peter has something in common with both Apollo and Marsyas, with art as transcendent illusion, and with the necessary submission to suffering by which the artist gains his laurels. Peter, however, Apollonian in his attraction to the light and clarity of Vermeer, rejects the print, recognising only in passing that it 'seemed to contain a message for me which I did not wish to read' (125/115).

With relief, Peter escapes from the surgery and into a cinema: 'My world, with all its oppressive detail of pain and inconsequence was behind me' (138/127). In the movie, *Young Man With A Horn*, a celebration of musical success based on the life of Bix Beiderbecke, the musical artist triumphs by rising above his erotic desires, fighting free of a corrupt woman (Lauren Bacall) to fall into the arms of the 'good artistic woman' (139/128), played by Doris Day. After 'the great glaring planetary visions' (140/128) of the film, Peter is unwilling to come down from his heights. The meagre faces in the street displease him, and he is repelled by the blacks of Alton, whom he identifies fearfully as Dionysian 'wizards, possessing the black secrets of love and song' (140/129). Rejoining his father, who appears haloed by a streetlight as if in a Vermeer (149/137), he is accosted by a drunk, readily identifiable in his vinous complexion, 'splashed with purple' (157/143) as Dionysos. Far from observing Peter's father as a Vermeer, the leering drunk assumes he is a pederast. Though the major focus of the encounter is George, who learns from the drunk that he does not wish to die, and emerges from despair, Peter also gains a fresh draught of life. Dionysos is not a stable referent here. The drunk's appearance indicates the need for a conjunction of the two aesthetics. Clad in layers of scraps, 'shingled in rags' (156/143), he appears flayed, and his hair, standing out from his head like the rays of the sun, is iconographically Apollonian. After the encounter Peter positively welcomes renewed contact with ordinary people. 'Their existing at all exhilarated me, came to me as a blessing and a permission to live myself' (160/146).

Subsequent plot events underline the necessity for the artist to learn from both Dionysos and Apollo. While Peter's enforced sojourn in Alton, the result of an automobile breakdown, has its nightmarish qualities, it also provides him with an opportunity to re-enter existence. Two other artist-figures feature prominently – Hummel (Vulcan) the craftsman of the garage-forge, and Johnny Dedman, mechanical wizard, star-pupil of Industrial Arts, the Daedalus of the novel, who inhabits the labyrinthine booths of Minor Kretz's Minoan lunchroom. On one level, the successive automobile breakdowns indicate that Peter is no Prometheus. He is unable to coax a spark from the engine, and is finally defeated by a fault in the actual body of the car. The incidents also suggest that less transcendent, practical arts have their own value. Peter himself recognises this: 'if I had not wanted so badly to be Vermeer, I would have tried to be Johnny Dedman' (123/114).

Johnny Dedman also forces Peter to confront the erotic mysteries of the body. In a surrealistic sequence, in which Peter as Prometheus chained to his rock receives a series of visits from the townspeople, Dedman displays a pack of pornographic playing cards. At first Peter is slow to comprehend. The phallic ace of spades is only 'an apple with a thick black stem' (180/164). In the development, however, the Jack of hearts (a '69' configuration) appears suddenly 'beautiful, a circle completed, a symmetry found, a sombre whirlpool of flesh' (181/165). The scene evolves into a Latin class in which Peter stumblingly translates a lyrical celebration of the beauty of the naked Venus. On his rock, Peter confronts the horror which the body can inspire, in Arnie Werner's hostile comments on his psoriasis. Yet he also learns of its possible beauty. This imagistic discovery of the body is followed by actual exposure. When Peter shows his psoriasis to Penny he appears 'half-skinned' and feels 'like a slave ready for flogging, or like that statue of the Dying Captive which Michelangelo did not fully release from the stone' (245/222). Penny's tender acceptance suggests that in this scene Peter reveals his imagined ugliness and is loved for his inner self. Though he cannot rise from his rock to transcend the suffering of life, he may yet learn to accept it. Outside, nature reasserts itself. Snow descends in tiny flakes, and a skin of beauty is laid over the earth. Marooned by the snow, Peter and George are forced to take refuge with Hummel and his wife Vera. Vera is the Venus of the novel, 'a woman of overarching fame; legends concerning her love-life circulated like dirty coins in the student underworld' (276/249). In Vera's home, Peter's easy transcendental certainties collapse. Reading an article on the proofs for the existence of God, he has a moment of panic as he realises that there are none (277/250). He turns towards Vera as a woman who 'serves to make horror habitable' (277/250). That Peter is now able to accept erotic woman is also suggested in his subsequent conversation with his father. As they walk home, George observes Venus in the sky. Peter's potentially new direction is indicated in his question: 'Can you steer by it?' (285/257). In addition Peter now recognises the selflessness of his father's love. In the struggle with the car's snow chains, Peter is symbolically set free from his rock. George flings away the chains, which make a hole in the snow which 'suggests a fallen bird' (261/235). In the Prometheus myth, Chiron, the centaur, redeems the crime of Prometheus by sacrificing his own immortality. Prometheus is set free and the eagle departs. In accepting death (in the novel a living death as an impoverished schoolteacher) George Caldwell sets his son free. At the close of the novel the red shirt is flung aside, like 'a flayed hide stiff with blood' (292/263). Contemplating the Pennsylvania landscape Peter submits to nature:

> I burned to paint it, just like that, in its puzzle of glory; it came upon me that I must go to Nature disarmed of perspective and stretch myself like a large transparent canvas upon her in the hope that, my submission being perfect, the imprint of a beautiful and useful truth would be taken.   (293/264)

Flayed, suffering, accepting the body and the puzzle of nature, Peter the adolescent is set free to become an artist of a less transcendent type.

In the light of Peter's evolution, the overall form of the novel takes on a special significance. Much critical effort has been expended upon the two major structural problems which the novel presents: the intermingling of a Greek mythological apparatus with the realistically depicted Pennyslvania of 1947,

and the unusual narration in which Peter's first person memories
alternate with the story of his father, presented in scenic terms by
an objective narrator. Formally the novel thus opposes a static,
scenic, 'shining illusion' to a narrative bound to time. Though
Peter is only the subjective narrator in three chapters, it may be
that his major work is the narrative, rather than his paintings. It
is, after all, Peter himself who registers doubts about the quality of
the latter, and perceives his own degeneration. Where the
paintings are abstract, the novel is not. Larry E. Taylor has
established that the structure of the novel is designed to mirror the
poetic convention of the pastoral elegy, including four short
chapters in a formal or lyrical style, which involve stock language,
song and the conventional jargon of journalism. Chapter III, in
which Chiron teaches the children of the gods, celebrates the
hero's beauty in life and includes the conventional catalogue of
flowers and herbs, and the paean, or heroic hymn. Chapter V, an
obituary in the manner of a small-town newspaper, forms a
conventional expression of communal grief. Personal grief
dominates Chapter VIII, in which Peter composes a lament, and
an elegiac interrogation of the universe as to the meaning of death.
Chapter IX, with its emphasis on consolation, involves George's
acceptance of death, culminating in a brief epilogue, recording the
centaur's apotheosis, as he is translated to immortality among the
stars. The novel therefore constitutes a memorialisation of George
Caldwell, and a wide-ranging interrogation of death in lyric
rather than philosophical terms, amply fulfilling Kierkegaard's
recommended aesthetic treatment of death. Though George is, to
some extent, a figure in a canvas, his position as Chiron, half-man,
half-horse, emphasises the liminality of the human condition, on
the threshold between gods and beasts, caught between the
timeless and the timebound. The paradoxical nature of man's
situation, the collision between human and divine, the
universality of suffering are thus communicated indirectly but
fully. Though George is apotheosised, he is only in part a god, and
Peter thus admits the conflict between gods and world, between
metaphysics and aesthetics. Myth therefore functions as both an
illusion to be penetrated and as a compensation for the horrors of
existence. As a human being Peter Caldwell enjoys only an
ambiguous, subjective understanding of the gods and their
creation, just as, as a narrator, he remains in problematic relation
to his story, which combines the formal clarity of the Apollonian

with a full confrontation of Dionysian darkness. As an artist Peter learns not to transcend life but to exist within it. The highly self-conscious metafictional structure of *The Centaur* thus calls attention to the novel as a work of fiction, not of metaphysics.

In his introduction to the Czech edition of *Of the Farm* Updike indicated that the work had connections with its predecessor:

> In a sense this novella is *The Centaur* after the centaur has died; the mythical has fled the ethical, and a quartet of scattered survivors grope with their voices toward cohesion. And seek to give each other the stern blessing of freedom mentioned in the epigraph from Sartre. (*Picked-Up Pieces*, p. 83)

The epigraph in question is directly concerned with the existential nature of freedom, quoting Sartre's dictum that 'a man is a being in whom existence precedes essence', a free being who can desire only his own freedom. In consequence, Sartre can 'want only the freedom of others'. *Of the Farm* confronts the difficulties involved, firstly in granting others the freedom of their own subjective conceptions without becoming trapped or ossified within these conceptual systems, and secondly in maintaining a sense of self which the fictions of others threaten to dissolve. The novella places equal emphasis upon the individual discourses of four characters, each expressing their own personal mythology of the world. Updike described it (*Picked-Up Pieces*, p. 83) as chamber music for four voices, which echo each other's phrases and themes, take turns dominating, embark on brief narrative solos, and recombine in argument or harmony. Though one of the four, Joey Robinson, is the first-person narrator, he has no special narrative authority. Indeed the novella records his struggle to maintain his voice against the engulfing voices of others, rather than validating his discourse as dominant.

Returning to his mother's farm with his second wife Peggy and her son Richard, Joey is alarmed to discover himself enshrined and ossified. The walls are covered in pictures and mementoes of his earlier self: 'I was so abundantly memorialized that it seemed I must be dead' (15/17). His mother's only concession to Peggy's presence is to replace a portrait of his first wife Joan with an idyllic little landscape, expressive of her own idealised mythology of the farm. Uninterested in actually working her property, Mrs Robinson takes an essentialist stance to the farm. For her it has value in its being, rather than in what it might become. She emphasises a Platonic, transcendent aesthetic in which the farm figures as a sacred place. Reading in her personal book of nature, Mrs Robinson invests the universe with intentions and meanings (23/24), personalising nature in an ideal pastoral sense. Her language thus becomes as much of a threat to Joey as her pictures. Where Joey describes himself as able to tolerate only to a limited degree 'the pressure of the unspoken' (61/57), his mother is 'infinitely at home in the realm of implication, where everything can be revised' (61/57). Effectively Joey has already been revised to fit his mother's conceptions. At one point he is startled to hear 'how Joan and my earlier self had become part of my mother's saga of the farm' (25/26). To maintain the mythology which she has made of her life, Mrs Robinson uses language in extremely subtle ways, performing feats of careful circumvention and paradoxical linkage, employing nuance and analogy in the service of her myth. Peggy, however, penetrates these illusions mercilessly. When Mrs Robinson entertains a fantasy of her farm as a 'people sanctuary' (71/65), co-opting Richard in the process, Peggy comments that the emphasis on weeding out the diseased makes her sanctuary sound more like a concentration camp. One individual's freedom is another's entrapment. In contrast to Mrs Robinson's idealising emphasis, Peggy expounds 'her own mythology, of women giving themselves to men, of men in return giving women a reason to live' (31/31). Where Mrs Robinson thinks that in moving Joey to the farm she saved him from social tameness, freeing him to become a poet, Peggy argues (112/101) that only *she* has allowed him the freedom to be himself, by accepting him as he is. In his first marriage, to Wordsworthian Joan (109/98) Joey had acted on his mother's transcendent directives rather than his own.

Joey's initial response to the clash between idealising mother and earthy wife is to attempt to insert Peggy into his mother's myth. In a lyrical meditation he converts her into a walking pastoral. His wide-hipped Nebraskan wife thus yields 'a variety of landscapes' (46/44), a rolling perspective of cotton bolls, a taut vista of mesas, Antarctica, a French castle on a hill, and a receding valley land. These painterly visions, which transform Peggy into a picture, much as his mother's pictures capture him, none the less prove a signal failure when Joey learns that Peggy has slept with her former husband. Peggy's quasi-Lawrentian creed of the body is fine in the abstract, but gives Joey pause when he discovers that this woman actually has given herself to a specific man. Importantly, Joey is quite content to accept the existence of her previous lovers, but not her husband. 'The others aren't real' to him (94/85) whereas McCabe is.

Joey's first attempt, as husband, to fence his wife in, culminating in his comment, 'My wife is a field' (59/55), founders when reality undercuts his pastoral illusion. An alternative means of approaching the conflicts of the farm is propounded in a sermon from the local pastor. In his discourse, a Barthian exposition of the proper Christian relation between the sexes, the preacher dwells on Adam's first action, naming the beasts of the field:

> Is not language an act of husbandry, a fencing-in of fields?. . . .
> Language aerates the barren density of brute matter with the
> penetrations of the mind, of the spirit.   (151/134)

A succession of internal fictions, attached to Richard, correlates to the action of the novella and serves to reconcile Joey to the shifts and sleights of language. At one point Mrs Robinson offers to provide Richard with a nature book to help him identity the flora of the farm. Joey's comment, that he personally 'could never match the pictures up with the real things exactly. The ideal versus the real' (64/59), sums up the essence of his problem in philosophical terms. Richard's response lays the blame elsewhere, on the 'lousy pictures' (64/59). The clash between real and ideal is the underlying theme in three 'fictions-within-the-fiction', which are related by Richard and Joey. Richard is an enthusiastic reader of science fiction. In the first such tale, the reader discovers that what was apparently the future turns out to be the distant past. On one level the story mirrors Joey's fear of ossification, caught in his mother's image of the past. Defensively, Joey expounds the scientific basis of the story. Richard, however, resents the fact that the fantasy 'which had seemed solely his, had been appropriated by real life' (54/50). Joey's rationalising, objective comment dispels the power of the narrative. The second story features a boy with a gigantic intellect who, at the age of 18 months, reads the dictionary through to learn the language. Richard's joke, 'But then can he match the words to the real things?' (65/60), underlines his unease with the ambiguities of language. In one respect the story relates to Richard, who had thought to read the nature book from cover to cover and thus to know and name nature. He is corrected by Mrs Robinson, who emphasises that subjective experience is essential to knowledge: 'You don't know the plants until you see them really' (121/108). On another level the story relates to Joey. At its close the boy becomes a cretin. In an ironic demonstration of Einstein's concept of relativity, the boy's reverse progression is akin to 'the line that comes back on itself from underneath' (108/97) in curved space. Where the first story demonstrates the iron grip of the past, the second emphasises the dissolution of the self. Joey comes uncomfortably close to the boy as he sees the discourses of his two women, each emanating from the relative position of the observant speaker, dissolving his certainties and effacing his sense of self.

Joey, however, is able to offer a correction fiction of his own invention, a bed-time story about a frog. Hearing rumours of a wonderful treasure deep in his guts, the frog sets out to discover it, descending the stairs of his head, the ladder of his ribs, until, as he goes further and further into himself, he disappears. Joey's identification with the frog is suggested when he describes it spearing a 'poor fly' (129/116), and remembers 'poor Joan'. Eager to rejoin his wife and mother, whose voices reach him indistinctly from below, Joey hastens to complete the story. The frog's disappearance becomes a hibernating period, ending as the frog ascends to his eyes, throws open the windows of his lids, and gazes out on a blue sky. Several readers have interpreted the fable as registering the danger of losing the spiritual (the sky) in the pursuit of physical or sexual treasure (in the guts). The story, however, also articulates Joey's own recognition of the dangers of solipsistic fantasy and the benefits of language. The frog's return to the world from his search for evanescent treasure within the self indicates Joey's desire to penetrate illusion and to be active in existence. Descending his own stairs, Joey pauses. A scent in the air suggests 'some nostalgic treasure' (132/118), but proves to be only the perfume of Peggy's damp hair. Recognising that nostalgic treasure is an illusion (his mother's) he has also learned that immersion in the body (Peggy's myth) is not an absolute value either. In an indirect, paradoxical fashion the story expresses subjectively something which Joey is unable to formulate in objective terms. Language mediates the real and the ideal in ways inaccessible to more abstract media, just as the tale of the frog, a free invention, communicates more fully to Richard than the objective and rational bases of science fiction.

Downstairs Joey finds his wife and mother arguing. Unable to reconcile their warring viewpoints, he reflects:

> Perhaps they were both right. All misconceptions are themselves data which have the minimal truth of existing in at least one mind. Truth, my work had taught me, is not something static. . . . Rather, truth is constantly being formed from the solidification of illusions. (135/120)

The reference to Joey's work holds its own ironies. In his profession in advertising, Joey fosters collective illusion in manipulative terms. Though his particular speciality is 'corporate image presentation' (109/98), he proves quite unable to form one image out of the fabulous countersystems of his two women. By recognising subjectivity as truth he grants them the freedom to propound their own respective myths, while avoiding enslavement to either. Rather than forming one syncretic image of the farm, Joey has to learn to transpose it into language which permits ambiguities and paradoxes to remain. At the end of the novella, after his mother's mild heart attack, Joey finds the farm deserted. No longer 'a lush and fabled haven' (160/142), it has become a wild and dangerous place, 'a vacuum pulling into itself madmen and rapists' (160/142). Peggy is discovered crouching in the bushes, terrorised by a passing carload of men. As his mother's pastoral image of the farm as sanctuary is exploded, so Peggy's bodily confidence also evaporates. Each character moves, if momentarily, out of illusion and towards truth. Reconciled to his wife, Joey strokes her spine which he feels as a description of grief.

> as in those new paintings whose artists, returning to nature from the realm of abstraction, render a sky an impossible earth-red which nevertheless answers to our eyes as sky. (162/144)

He thus accepts that earthy Peggy answers to his needs, though she is not drawn to the ideal specifications of his mother's pastoral image. Reconciliation with his mother also implies reconciliation with her language. When Mrs Robinson tells him to sell the farm, Joey decides to answer in our old language, our only language, allusive and teasing that, with conspirational tact declared nothing and left the past apparently unrevised.

'Your farm?' I said. 'I've always thought of it as our farm.'   (172/154)

Whether, by 'our', Joey means that the farm belongs to him and his mother, or to him and his wife, remains a productive ambiguity.

In its emphasis on language, *Of the Farm* draws upon Kierkegaard's defence of art as a process of communication in which paradox and ambiguity may be sustained and the problematics of existence fully confronted. It is however in *Marry Me* that Updike proceeds to his most searching exploration of the aesthetic realm. Most obviously the plot hinges upon a problem of choice. After an initial spiritual crisis which exhibits Kierkegaardian 'dread' at its most acute, Jerry Conant escapes from the fear of death into an illusory idyll with Sally, the wife of Richard Mathias. Jerry's ethical capacity, the ability to make decisions, is well-nigh nonexistent. Unable to decide whether to remain with his wife Ruth or to abandon her for his lover, Jerry vacillates intolerably. At successive points he allows the decision to be put off because Ruth tells him to stay, because to marry Sally would be to convert their ideal love into drab reality, because he is able to board a plane, because his children may suffer, because Ruth survives an accident, because Sally goes to Florida, because Ruth may be pregnant. Though Jerry is ostensibily Christian, he avoids action through the fear of suffering, in favour of sidestepping choice altogether, converting external circumstances into the word of God, and surrendering his will to a private illusion of heaven in Sally's arms. Sally and Richard are described in terms which clearly suggest Kierkegaard's aesthetic sphere. As Sally reflects, 'Jerry believed in choices, in mistakes, in damnation, in the avoidance of suffering. She and Richard believed simply that things happened' (45/43). Hedonistic and greedy for life, the Mathiases live for the present. Ruth, however, is 'aesthetic' in a different sense. For all her emphasis on the need for decision and on the moral dimensions of the affair, she none the less inhabits the aesthetic sphere. (As we shall see, the Conants' art-school background is important in this respect.) Between the two poles of Christian Jerry and atheist Richard, the two women represent different mediating aesthetics. Where Sally is over-involved in the immediate and external, Ruth uses a sense of style to detach herself too far from events, keeping herself at one remove from existence.

The Kierkegaardian theme also influences the form of the work. Uneasy about the book's 'lack of sociology'[20] Updike gave it the subtitle 'A Romance' to underline the less realistic nature of the work. In its structure this romance emphasises the subjectivity of each character, with individual chapters ostensibly presented from the point of view of one protagonist. A short first section, *Warm Wine*, from Jerry's perspective, is followed by *The Wait* (centred on Sally), *The Reacting of Ruth* and *The Reacting of Richard*, culminating in a fifth chapter in which three possible endings are produced for the reader's inspection (Jerry with Sally, Jerry with Ruth, Jerry alone). Choice is therefore the energising factor in the plot, the structure presents a choice of alternative subjective viewpoints, and in the triple ending that choice is extended out to the reader. In addition a plethora of images of mirrors, reflections, eyes, paintings, photographs, and other works of art, foregrounds the problematic nature of art and of the individual perspective on reality.[21]

The novel begins with a brief, apparently idyllic tryst between Sally and Jerry. While Jerry dwells on the shortness of their time together, Sally invites him to have faith in the beauty of the present, promulgating a creed of simplicity and immediacy, and presenting herself as lacking inner existence:

> 'I am simple. I'm just like' – similes were hard for her, she so instinctively saw things as themselves – 'that broken bottle. I have no secrets.' (11/15)

Jerry leaps at the bait. With Sally he appears to enjoy a perfect continuity of nature and feeling, which he transposes into Edenic terms. The dunes around him appear like 'clean-swept nature, never tasted' (5/10), and Sally's 'simple and quick' (10/14) lovemaking takes on a prelapsarian innocence. Eagerly Jerry casts them as 'the original man and woman' (7/12), in their unspoiled 'perfect place' (4/10) amidst the dunes. He even applauds Sally's tendency to avoid making moral distinctions: 'You think Moravia is good, you think warm wine is good, you think lovemaking is good' (11/15). Ironies, however, surround the couple. The perfect paradisal place is not easily relocated on subsequent visits. The serpentine access road, with its ambiguous forks and unexplained turnings, leads to an area of hollows which is 'deceptively complex' (4/10). For the reader, doubts as to the virtues of simplicity are also raised by the inanity of the lovers' exchanges. ('Hey?' 'Hi.' 'Hi.' is one such.) Jerry affects an adolescent manner of speech, mixed of hip slang and calf-love monosyllables, and has developed a taste for corny popular songs. One such, 'Born to Lose', which contains the line, 'Every dream has only brought me pain', signals its own ironic counterpoint to Sally's singing, inflected monosyllables. As Jerry casts Sally as his heaven-on-earth, Sally herself ceases to be more than an accessory and adjunct to his personal illusion. When making love, her face becomes 'a mirror held inches below his own face, a misted mirror more than another person' (10/15).

In the second chapter, *The Wait*, Sally passes through the mirror into a looking-glass world of a very different type. Her impulsive trip to Washington is an attempt to repeat a previous romantic meeting. Though aware that 'it would never happen again, never happen the same' (22/25), she none the less flies after Jerry, to insist that 'I'm here with you, and everything else seems very far away' (30/31). For Sally, living in immediacy, the past is meaningless: 'a dingy pedestal erected so she could be alive in this moment' (26/27). Her belief in the present is, however, undercut, both in the structure of the chapter and in its imagery. The whole of the second visit is permeated with memories of the preceding, the narrative weaving between past and present, so that the reader is provided with a double temporal perspective. In addition, the Kierkegaardian 'aesthetic' nature of Sally's existence is foregrounded. Significantly, Sally's planned excuse for her absence from home is attendance at an art-appreciation course. In a sense, Washington provides just such an educative experience, but not on Sally's own terms. Jerry's idea of a romantic experience involves a visit to a museum to see some Vermeers. In the museum, Sally enjoys a moment of inner expansion: 'The gigantic scale of the rotunda did not seem inhuman but right: our inner spaces warrant palaces' (36/36). Studying Leoni's sculpture of Charles V, she 'existed as a queen in his hyperthyroid gaze' (36/36). The imagery, however, conveys a growing sense of unreality. Sally becomes 'conscious of existing among paintings, of shining in portraits' eyes . . . of posing in a rapt and colourful theatre' (37/37). For Sally, immersed in the aesthetic sphere, the world becomes less an area for qualitative inner transformation (a process which art may assist) than a hall of mirrors reflecting her own solipsistic sense of self, a variegated theatre in which she occupies the starring role. Her attitude of passive observation transforms Washington into a gigantic illusion, composed of 'frosted' (26/28) federal buildings, a 'marzipan' (26/28) Capitol, and a White House 'made of brilliant fake stuff, like meringue (26/28). The appetitive imagery suggests one gigantic illusory wedding-cake. (Marriage is on Sally's greedy mind.) Strolling through the stage set of Washington, amidst crowds of other tourists, Sally converts everyone into an admiring audience, imagining that statues are trying to catch her attention, that all the men are eyeing her, that she is 'reflected in every glance and glass entryway' (34/34).

The aesthetic, in the more usual sense, offers a corrective perspective. In their hotel room, the couple have made love beneath the disapproving gaze of 'small-mouthed, fastidious' (32/32) Holbein portraits. Seeing herself through the portraits' eyes Sally envisages their erotic encounter as just one more in a series of drunken and adulterous couplings. Previously Sally had delighted in the simplicity of sexuality. Now she recalls how, on her honeymoon, she had looked into the mirrors in her Paris room and 'seen the truth of it; people were like animals' (47/45). When Jerry tells her that he prefers her to Ruth on her animal merits, the phrase stings. In the museum lunchroom she is suddenly repelled by the Audubon prints of predatory birds which surround them. These works of art suggest that Sally is acting simply in an animal fashion, not in a way which gives shape or meaning to existence.

Where *Warm Wine* presented a mock-heaven, *The Wait* transports the lovers to a more infernal environment. When Jerry arranges to meet Sally in Washington, he tells her 'I'd know you in hell' (25/27). The consequences of Sally's creed become apparent in the subsequent wait at the airport. Jerry had described Sally as 'like a set of golden stairs I can never finish climbing' (46/44), associating her with the radiance of heaven. At the airport, unable to fly, he wonders whether their love would survive if he 'destroyed my wife and waded through my children's blood for you' (45/43). Earlier Sally had reminisced happily about her youthful pleasure in gambling at the racecourse. Now, becalmed by an airline strike, she finds herself at the mercy of chance,

condemned to an endless present in which the extra hours gained
with Jerry produce only tedium and misery. Abruptly her sense of
herself as the centre of the world collapses. It dawns on her that
the agitation in the airport lounge does not centre upon her.
Misery is general. Other people and their problems exist. The
impression of a no-man's land between destinations, where people
are subject to an arbitrary authority, provides a hideous reverse
image of Sally's existence in terms of fortune and external
circumstances. At several points the crowds of would-be
passengers take on the appearance of souls in Limbo or purgatory.
Access to the plane is barred by an employee with an expression of
'angelic scorn' (48/46). When an announcement interrupts the
Muzak ('Easter Parade') a 'serene parade' (48/46) of those with
reservations passes through the gate, followed by two standby
passengers, 'the mysterious elect' (49/46). Jerry and Sally, their
entry barred, are forced back into 'Pandemonium' (57/53). At
each announcement, the mob 'scenting redemption' (68/62) press
forward, only to be pushed back, packed tightly together and
smelling of panic like cattle in a chute (47/45). The gate is tightly
shut, 'like a gas-chamber' (48/45), and the floor angled 'as if to
drain blood' (48/45). Out of the crowd an acquaintance appears,
A. D. ('Anno Domini') Wigglesworth, aptly named for the author
of *The Day of Doom*. While Jerry scurries to and fro in the
rats-passages of labyrinthine corridors, Sally's reaction is to wish
herself away, plunging into a novel. Ironically it is an existentialist
work, by Camus, which Sally sees as 'unreality' (42/41).
Resigning herself passively, she informs Jerry that 'whatever is
possible will be fine' (42/41).

In contrast Jerry understands the wider implications of their
situation. In conversation with Sally he draws from her the
admission that he is torturing her with his indecision, that her
present unhappiness is only part of her continual suffering, not
accidental and temporary. He draws two conclusions. Firstly he
recognises that to possess Sally in marriage would destroy their
love. Realisation would cancel its ideal dimension. The
surrounding context bears him out. Earlier Sally had diagnosed
Jerry's fatal flaw as his inability to remain fixed in the role of lover
as she had imagined it. Instead, by acting like a husband, he had
become 'unreal' (16/20). By going to Washington Sally intends to
fix Jerry back in that ideal role. She refuses, for example, to help
him choose toys for his children, lest the saleswoman take her for

his wife. In the airport, however, Sally becomes heartily sick of love (60/58). Her mechanical conversation with Wigglesworth makes her feel like a whore, and she envies the bridesmaid en route to a wedding, who gains a plane seat ahead of her. She even finds herself forced to impersonate 'Mrs Conant' to the employees. The enforced wait therefore transforms Sally momentarily into a wife, and the experience supports Jerry's diagnosis of the unrealisable, illusory quality of their love.

Jerry also draws a second conclusion from his sense of the bind in which he finds himself:

> To live without you is death to me. On the other hand, to abandon my family is a sin; to do it I'd have to deny God, and by denying God I'd give up all claim to immortality. (52/55)

For all Sally's scorn for Jerry's easy absolutes, the observation suggests that Jerry is aware of a fundamental clash between immediate pleasure with Sally and eternal life, between the aesthetic and the religious spheres. Jerry's ability to make an ethical decision, however, remains strictly in abeyance. Since it appears that there are no more flights, he proposes marriage: 'We can't go back. God has spoken' (67/61). But when an offer of a seat materialises, Jerry, flooded with relief, lurches explosively away from Sally. A contented sky-pilot, he retires back into his illusions. As their plane rises into the heavens, his italicised interior monologue recapitulates his blasphemous dream of Sally as heavenly: 'Through the strait gate between your legs I had entered this firmament' (70/64). Beneath him the inferno of Washington is transfigured into an aesthetic paradise: 'Dante could not have dreamed such a rose' (69/73).

After the idyll and counter-idyll of *Warm Wine* and *The Wait*, the third chapter, *The Reacting of Ruth*, presents the aesthetic sphere in a different sense. Where Sally's experiences in Washington suggest that the work of art may provide opportunities for inward growth, indicating longer and larger perspectives than those afforded by the immediate present, Ruth's reactions imply that art may also offer a dangerously easy means of disengaging from reality, or of distancing it altogether. As the chapter opens Ruth is pondering two photographs which offer a reprise of previous events. The first, a colour print, celebrates a religious occasion, the baptism of Geoffrey. Though Jerry had gone to great lengths to have his child christened, he himself is absent, figuring in the picture only as a purple shadow in one corner. Ruth has contrasted Jerry's nonchalant attitude to his family with that of Richard, who sees the raising of children as a problem. Jerry, however, feels no such anxiety: 'he was the original, and in the children God had made some reproductions which in time would be distributed. Jerry loved duplication and its instruments – cameras, printing presses' (83/74). Reproductive responsibility has been firmly left with God. For Ruth, on the other hand, what is significant in the photograph is 'What does not show' (76/68): Joanna's reaction to the baptism, Ruth's own misery at acceding to a religious ritual which she cannot approve, her absent husband. Though Jerry is the photographer and has even taken care to pose the family against a brightly coloured crocus, he ignores the fact that his subjects are thoroughly miserable, Ruth tired and drawn, Joanna apprehensive, the boys uncomfortable in their Sunday best. In contrast, the second photograph, taken by Sally, captures Jerry in black and white, on an idyllic fishing trip with the Mathiases. Recalling the day, Ruth remembers their greedy feasting on mussels, registering the Mathiases as repellent in their 'determined hedonism' (80/71). In the picture, Jerry appears 'harshly shadowed and curiously savage' (80/72), 'cruel' and alone. In little, the two photographs encapsulate two opposed aesthetic visions – the one a colourful celebration of a religious moment, engineered by a distant Jerry, the other a darker, more shadowy image of Jerry, immersed in immediate hedonism.

Informed by her contemplation of the photographs, Ruth now re-assesses her marriage. The Conants had met in the ideal realm of an art school: 'Naively immersed in the cult of true colour, of vital line. They adored the silent gods of the museum-temple' (72/69). When they first saw each other naked it was 'as if a new object of art had been displayed to each, and their marriage carried forward this quirk of detachment' (76/69). Significantly, the opposition in the two photographs of colour and sharper line forms an analogy to their different painterly styles. Ruth's paintings had been 'remarkably unafraid' (76/69). No Kierkegaardian dread for Unitarian Ruth whose amorphous faith has been reduced to two tenets: not to cause suffering deliberately, and to take pleasure in each day (78/70). Though her paintings are deficient in perspective, they show a rare touch for colour in all its immediacy. In contrast Jerry's gift is for line and outline. Each subject he paints becomes 'a kind of over-animated ghost, wherein swerve and energetically "worked" detail replaced the dense and placid life of substance' (76/69). Where Ruth captures the physical substance of reality but lacks a structured vision, Jerry spiritualises substance into ghostly outlines, skimming over the realities of existence. Although their styles appear to be complementary, the one remedying the defaults of the other, Ruth now feels that 'their merger was perhaps too easy, too aesthetic' (7/69). In their subsequent marriage, 'unexpected shadows deepened' (77/69).

The insufficiencies of such an aesthetic pairing are confirmed in later events. Ruth and Jerry collaborate to maintain their distance through aesthetic strategies. When Jerry suspects that Ruth has a lover, he gazes into space, 'as if at an aesthetic problem' (91/80). When Ruth abandons her affair she finds no recognition from Jerry of her renewed commitment to her marriage: 'She had stood before the mirror of their marriage and was given back – nothing' (96/85). Suspecting erroneously that Jerry knows, she finds him obliviously reading *Art News*: 'Again, the mirror had looked through her' (98/86). Though Ruth has begun to distrust the aesthetic emphasis, the discovery of Jerry's affair propels her back onto familiar ground. When eventually he drops his bombshell, Ruth's defensive reaction is to restyle her perception of her husband. He becomes 'beautiful, a statue out of reach . . . a medieval Adam' (114/99), while her son Geoffrey, his security threatened, takes on the distorted angles of a Picasso. Where Sally is aesthetic in living for immediate enjoyment, Ruth uses her artistic education as a protective device. At especially painful moments she always retreats into art. Jerry, menacing in bed, becomes a Goya; Sally, violently tinted in the sun's glare, a Bonnard. Jerry, trying to comfort Charlie against his impending departure, is framed in a doorway 'as if in one of the domestic Dutch masters' (179/152). Geoffrey, after Jerry's departure, becomes 'a stolen masterpiece in marble' (194/164). In what should be an explosive confrontation with Sally, Ruth takes refuge in a sarcastic assessment of Sally's deficient décor, noting framed prints by 'mediocrities like Buffet and Wyeth' (126/109). She even observes her coffee-cup dispassionately as a Bonnard. Clearly there is some justice in Sally's charge that 'You mustn't just sit there and be amused. You must take responsibility for your actions, Ruth' (129/111). Though Ruth in turn accuses Sally of striking an attitude, entitling her final pose, on the lawn clutching her children, 'The Invader Repelled', Sally's counter-accusation is also validated: 'You and Jerry have been living too long up on that little arty cloud of yours' (134/115). In a sense the two women have transformed their conflict into a war of styles.

When Sally reports this confrontation to Jerry, their telephone conversation becomes a communication of all the uncertainties, pain and ambiguities of their position. After Jerry hangs up, however, Ruth finds that she has been doodling all the time, squares interlocking with squares, their overlap carefully shaded. 'Light and dark were balanced, confused though she had been' (140/120). Studying the abstraction she wonders whether, abandoned, she might become an artist after all. Ironically the image underlines the extent to which Ruth attempts to control the four sided problem (Ruth, Jerry, Sally, Richard) in aesthetic terms. Coolly she considers whether to abandon her marriage. 'Such sacrifice would be simple, bold, pure, aesthetic' (143/122). Instead she transforms its erotic basis, plunging into sexuality. Where Jerry spiritualises his erotic activities, Ruth decides that 'it's my aesthetic duty to really enjoy it' (154/131).

The connection between Ruth's aesthetic detachment and her refusal to enter the ethical sphere of willed decisions is dramatised in her car accident. Angered by her discovery that Jerry and Sally are in communication, Ruth sets out to consult Richard. For Ruth Richard's glassed-in office presents an image of security. Ruth 'liked noises that could not touch her, she liked the sensation of being naked behind a frosted-glass door' (158/135). Through the glass of her windshield, she observes the surrounding trees as if in a painting, their vivid green that of Monet or Pissarro, the salmon pink flecks on the birch-trunks reminiscent of Cézanne. Hesitating to denounce Sally, she is pulled back by a 'series of images' (158/135) towards Greenwood. When her car skids off the road, however, Ruth enters a different green wood, that of the Van Huyten estate. When she tries to steer she is surprised to find that nothing answers her touch on the wheeel: 'It was as if she looked into a mirror that then turned transparent' (160/136). Out of touch with reality, unable to choose a direction, and lost to all sense of her own identity, Ruth gives up, lies down on the seat and closes her eyes. Skidding into the trees she is passive to the accident, surrendering herself to chance. When she reopens her eyes, the scene is presented as if she had passed through the frame and into the picture. The trees now appear with extreme clarity 'poised in a sharp space somewhat artificial, like the depth of a stereoscope, unnaturally fresh and clean' (161/137). Ruth's own dizziness is transferred into the external world, where the woods swerve about her 'with the unmoving motion of a scene painted on the awning of a carousel' (161/137). The suspicion lingers that Ruth, unable to determine which direction to take, has abandoned control over her actions to enter an aesthetic landscape instead, a green wood all her own. She even likens her final vision of the car, incongruously parked in the middle of the trees, to a Rousseau. Ruth's passivity is confirmed when Richard collects her from the police station. Rather than acquainting him with the facts, she allows him to assume that she has a lover. Richard's overtures are rejected in highly ironic terms. 'Stick to the facts,' he says. 'I get the picture.' Ruth's reply, 'You don't, as a matter of fact. That's what's so so killing' (163/143) evades the truth. Ruth has 'got the picture' only in aesthetic terms and refuses to put Richard in the picture at all. Symbolically the accident suggests that Ruth is passive to chance and to external circumstances, contemplating the world as a colourful aesthetic sphere.

When Jerry and Ruth revisit the scene of the crash, the gulf between Ruth's perception of events and their reality widens. Retelling the accident Ruth emphasises the Edenic beauty of the calm trees. 'At each rerun the images deepened in colour' (169/144). Jerry, however, sees through her fiction. The broken wall, the harsh scars on the trees, the rutted lines gouged in the earth do not coordinate with Ruth's description of gentle flight. While Jerry accuses Ruth of a general passivity ('You just lie down on the front seat and hope everything goes away' (171/145)) he seizes upon the accident to confirm his own irresponsibility. To her horror Ruth realises that Jerry had wanted her to die, to save him from the agonies of choice. Now that she has survived he assumes that God as spoken:

> I've been waiting, I suppose, for God to do something, and this was it. His way of saying that nothing is going to happen. Unless you and I make it happen. (171/146)

Jerry's own passivity wakes Ruth up. Each day when he returns home he asks, 'Did anything happen?' Whenever he says it, Ruth feels an urge to smash her fist through a windowpane. On one occasion, Ruth does make something happen, smashing a glass and blurting out the facts to her children. In effect, Ruth is forced to recognise that she has become trapped, by her indecision, in a world behind glass, a never-never land of art and illusion.

> The crack between her mind and the world, bridged by a thousand stitches of perception, had quite closed, leaving her embedded, as the white unicorn is a prisoner in the tapestry. (186/158)

Acknowledging that she has, in part, caused Jerry's adultery by her distant coldness, she admits that 'As a negative wills a print, she had willed Sally' (186/157). Now the problem of the affair 'must be discharged by some last act of her will' (186/158).

As a result of this understanding, Ruth gains in two senses. In the first place the world is restored to her. Telling Jerry to go, she descends from her heights, recognising the complexity of existence on 'the earth with its tangle of tiny lives and deaths, that from a distance appears a lawn but up close is unendurably confused and cruel' (196/165). At the beach, she notes that Long Island Sound is a blue that cannot be painted (198/167), darker than carbon, brighter than titanium white. Emerging from the aesthetic Ruth takes a willed decision. When she fears that she is pregnant, Jerry offers to return. Ruth, however, will no longer allow an accident to determine her existence and decides upon abortion. Jerry, eager to extricate himself from any moral involvement, protests that a previous miscarriage 'had been God's will. This would be our will' (199/168). The content of this decision may be distressing, but it is at least a choice. When Ruth awakens next day to find herself bleeding, her reaction indicates how far she has progressed from her earlier detachment. Gazing at blood, she experiences a clear perception: 'A kind of photograph had been developed in the night' (202/170). The punning identification, in the earlier pages of the chapter, between Jerry's children and photographic reproductions, now recurs, but this time Ruth is the developer. Ruth no longer has any illusions and relates the image firmly back to her own individual existence. 'In the manner of modern abstraction, what she held was not a hieroglyph or symbol of herself, it was herself' (202/170). Though Ruth has moved from the aesthetic to the ethical, she has not progressed to the religious sphere. In that respect she understands her Sunday morning bleeding as a 'blank announcement of emptiness' (202/170).

It is only in the final chapter that the war of art is recast as a religious conflict, between Christian Jerry and atheist Richard. Both structurally and thematically the chapter explores the proposition that a lack of religious understanding impoverishes art. Throughout *Marry Me* the protagonists' viewpoints have been successively presented without the use of first person narration, in order to emphasise subjectivity rather than subjectivism. Although the fourth chapter is entitled *The Reacting of Richard*, it is important to note that it is not presented from Richard's point of view. Dialogue predominates and at intervals italicised passages reveal the shape of Jerry's memories, so that though Richard reacts, he is seen at one remove and appears to lack inner existence. The technique apparently reflects Jerry's perception of Richard as appropriately one-eyed, an atheist who lacks a vital dimension on reality. For Richard

> things were just so, flat, with nothing further to be said about them; it was the world [Jerry] realized, as seen without the idea of God lending each thing a roundness of significance. (225/188)

In Jerry's loaded terms Richard can only react to external events; he is incapable of religious and existential action. The irony, however, is also directed at Jerry. In the novel Jerry has persistently looked for God to make all his decisions. In the event it is Richard, a devil's advocate, who understands events only in a social context of divorce settlements, child support and lawyers, who fulfils the desired role of decision-maker. When Richard sets out the terms of the two divorces, doodling figures on a pad, 'a great immaterial weight shifted, like a tissue page in a Bible, unmasking the details of an infernal etching' (226/189). The veil torn away, Jerry wakes to the awareness that in proposing to Sally he has condemned himself to 'an eternity of repetition through . . . sin' (238/199).

Ostensibly Jerry has made his choice, yet two final episodes, each involving art and artists, play a crucial role in reversing that decision. Firstly Jerry agrees to paint some posters for Ruth. Though Ruth tells him simply to repeat one design, without attempting to be original, he finds himself trying to make each poster funnier and better than the previous one. The impossibility of static repetition is revealed to him through art. Contemplating his wife's self-portrait, a deficient likeness, he understands that in this picture, to the best of her ability 'she had given herself to him' (254/212). Around him the voices of his soon-to-be-abandoned children take on a disturbing tone, as if in a drawing where perspective lapses (254/212). Implicitly Jerry recognises that the members of his family are not mere repetitions drawn to his ideal specifications, but have their own individual existence. This dawning realisation is completed by Sally, who has planned to rent a local painter's 'little fairy house' (277/231) for her idyll with Jerry. Instinctively Jerry loathes it. 'It was the house of a man who had stripped his mind clean of everything but himself, his needs, his body, his pride' (262/219). Jerry cannot now assume that aesthetic role. Understanding finally that he has been projecting his own idealising vision upon Sally, the scales fall from his eyes. 'As an actual wife or whatever, she stopped being an *idea* and for the first time I *saw* her' (284/236). Reconciling himself to suffering, parting from Sally, Jerry tastes in the air 'humiliation and disgrace, which is also, strangely, the taste of eternal life' (273/228). Groping towards explanations with Ruth he recognises that his affair was the product of his illusions, his desire to sidestep choice and suffering, and to have his heaven on earth. Though Ruth can never fulfil this ideal role for him, the distance between them is now registered, paradoxically, as an advantage. 'In their willingness to live parallel lay their weakness and their strength' (284/237).

Events do not end, however, on quite such a note of Christian certainty. Turning the page, the reader discovers Sally and Jerry in Wyoming, and assumes yet another change of heart. Earlier in the novel Jerry had imagined transporting Sally to the West as an aesthetic rebirth: 'In Wyoming, I'd take up painting again' (52/49). On arrival, inhaling the 'mythical western air' (288/240), Jerry registers the landscape in static, pictorial terms. A descriptive paragraph mirrors the sweep of his eye, from the unreal beauty of the clouds, finely outlined as if etched, all shape but lacking in substance, to the uninhabitable mountain peaks, and through the middle distance to the airfield below him, its markings 'symbols in a cumbersome language employed by a worldwide race of myopic giants' (289/241). The transcendent, insubstantial vision of an immediate heaven gives way to the reality of the present, as Jerry finds his responsibility for Sally 'claustrophobically complex' (291/242). In the background the eyes of theatrically clad cowboys express only 'cruel ennui' (290/241). As reality impinges, 'the desert around them and they with it, evaporated, vanished, never had been' (292/243). This particular resolution recapitulates the movement of chapters one and two, as an idyllic escape into a realm of illusion collapses. Interviewed in 1980, Updike commented that 'Wyoming had been established throughout the book as a fanciful paradise which they were never going to get to'[22] but that, after drilling home the 'real' resolution at the end of the preceding chapter, he had felt the need to reassert the concept of romance. One of his intentions in the novel was 'to show illusion as a component of our daily lives to which air and dreams are as essential as earth and blood' (*Hugging the Shore*, p. 857).

Where the first ending is mythically undated, the second occurs in November, as Jerry and Ruth disembark in Nice. Here the manner of presentation also undercuts the validity of Jerry's choice, suggesting a return to Ruth's aesthetic sphere, rather than to Sally's simple immediacy. Ruth views the Riviera as 'just like a painting' (294/245), Jerry notes that the taxi-driver's coat is a blue seen only in pictures, and even Joanna observes pictorial roadsigns with stately detachment. In addition the imagery suggests a fractured and distorted reality. Nice is 'a prism' (296/246), its air 'Cubistically portioned' (293/244), its strollers 'divided exactly into halves of shadow and light' (296/246). The suggestions of a return to the status quo, implicit in the parallels of light and shade which recall Ruth's doodles, are confirmed in the conjunction of colour and line. 'Europe was pellucid in colour and in drawing crowded' (294/245). Ruth and Jerry have gone to Nice to paint for six months, 'side by side' (294/244). When they catch sight of a woman who resembles Sally, they exchange startled glances, their expressions 'like the multiplication between two mirrors' (295/245). Though side by side, Ruth and Jerry may still be in a state of illusion. Their arrival at the airport is presided over by a phantom apparition of Marlene Dietrich. 'This ghost, this construct of light and shadow' (293/244) appears to be contemplating them benignly as fellow spirits.

In the third ending, dated in March, Jerry descends alone in the West Indies. Painting in France has not gone well and he and Ruth have returned early. Though Jerry is still registering the

world in aesthetic terms, it has lost much of its beauty. Here a low
hill looks dull, as if its colour had sunk into unprimed canvas, and
the houses are 'surrealistically spaced along a straight blank
street' (302/251). One exchange indicates how squarely Jerry is
back where he started. When a taxi-driver asks him to choose a
destination, between towns at opposite ends of the island, Jerry
vacillates, joking: 'So I can't go to both' (297/247). When the
driver insists on a decision, he hesitates: 'He had not expected
there to be a choice' (297/247). In at least one highly ironic sense,
the Caribbean is Jerry's 'perfect place'. Welcoming the 'tropical
manner of outwaiting everything' (298/247), Jerry surrenders his
will to the driver, passively acceding to a detour through the
mountains. '"Sure", he said. Submit. Forget' (298/248). To
American Jerry the left-hand drive of the traffic converts forward
motion into 'a miracle worked with mirrors' (298/248). Re-
entering Wonderland, emerging 'from the forest into the sky'
(299/248), his mind moves into a wholly imaginary party
conversation with Sally, and he passes once more into idyll.

> The existence of this place satisfied him that there was a
> dimension in which he did go, as was right, at that party, or the
> next, and stand, timid and exultant, above the downcast eyes of
> her gracious, sorrowing face, and say to Sally, *Marry
> Me.* (303/252)

The novel thus ends with its own italicised title, directing the
reader back to its beginning, just as the successive endings move
in a circle from idyll in Wyoming, to disenchantment, and thence
to a renewed illusion. Each ending forms a reprise of earlier
events, the idyll gone sour, Ruth's aesthetic realm, the avoidance
of choice, so that the structure of the final chapter reflects the
general structure of the novel. In addition each ending repeats
and varies components of the preceding: descent from a plane in
an exotic locale, a squashed taxi-ride, a puzzling encounter with
another language (the Indian's in Wyoming, French in Nice,
West Indian English) and a reality rendered in pictorial terms.
The overall effect is of a chapter which mirrors the novel and is
itself composed of mirrors. By structuring the novel as a hall of
mirrors, flashing reflections and illusions, Updike foregrounds the
problematic nature of art, preventing the reader from translating
the work into a revelation of the infinite within the finite, or a

religious tract. Aesthetics and metaphysics remain separate and art is validated as a process of communication of subjectivity. While the three endings offer the reader a choice, no authoritative direction is provided by the author. In his foreword to a special edition of *Marry Me* Updike described his intentions in terms which suggest both the complexity and the indirection of the artistic process, in which reality is simultaneously reflected and rendered opaque and problematic, together with a Kierkegaardian emphasis on the value of art in conveying these complexities, in relation to which critical and intellectual exposition must remain insufficient.

> A novel imitates reality in, among other aspects, a certain opacity, a proud opacity. It must come on not wearing its meaning on the sleeve of an introduction but embodying its meaning, or, rather, meaning its existence. . . . The artist's effort perhaps consists not in bringing a work to perfection but of bringing it to the point where the creation, not the creator, takes the active part in the sentence. (*Hugging the Shore*, p. 857)

A coda remains: *A Month of Sundays* (1975), quite the most metafictional and self-conscious of Updike's novels and easily his least popular.[23] In interview Updike expressed his own disappointment at finding it 'rather snippingly received. To me it was a kind of breakthrough.'[24] Though *A Month of Sundays* was published before *Marry Me* (1976) the composition of the latter spans a considerable period, with *The Wait* first published in the *New Yorker* in 1968, and *Warm Wine* in a special edition in 1973. Arguably, therefore, *A Month of Sundays* is later in inception and marks a new direction in style and theme. In a subtext running through the three preceding 'aesthetic' novels, Updike implicitly justified his own activity as a writer rather than as a graphic artist, his first ambition. In *A Month of Sundays* the pictorial is firmly left behind. The continued exploration of the division between body and spirit, already a central concern in *The Centaur* and *Of the Farm*, finds its focus in language, which is here both subject and method.

A Month of Sundays centres upon a writer in the process of writing. Thomas Marshfield, an adulterous preacher, composes a discursive journal from the desert motel to which he has been banished for a month by his scandalised flock. Reflecting upon his erotic exploits, Marshfield recapitulates his relationships with his wife Jane, and his mistresses Frankie and Alicia, among others, casting the three women as representative of good works, faith and the body. Throughout, the sustained analogy of writing and sexuality invites attention to the capacity of language (as of sex) to mediate between body and spirit. Like Joey Robinson, Marshfield originally wants things pinned down and secured in unambiguous terms. In reaction against his father's humanism he becomes a Barthian, and pins his faith on things as revealing the immanence of 'God' – an unambiguous term for him. 'Since before language dawned I knew what the word [God] meant: all haggling as to this is linguistic sophistry' (25/25).

Marshfield's attitude to language evolves in tandem with his erotic activities. First attracted to his wife at divinity school where her father was a professor of ethics, his courtship progresses in parallel ('as it were in running footnote' (51/46)) to the texts of her father's lectures. The course ends, 'as the logical positivists thought to end human confusion by careful reference to the dictionary' (54/49), and Marshfield promptly proposes. 'I introduced the word "marriage"' (54/49). For Marshfield the body is 'a swamp in which the spirit drowns' (46/42). With Jane, 'ethical' (49/44) but an unbeliever, he inhabits a grey area in which neither spirit nor body are fully satisfied. (In their courtship they stop short of sexual consummation, in favour of mutual masturbation.) From Jane, Marshfield escapes into the arms of Alicia, his organist, and a fresh discovery of the joys of the flesh. Alicia's sensuality, however, threatens to swamp the Word altogether. Marshfield's sermons are reduced to marginal interruptions to Alicia's increasingly prolonged performances on the organ. When his adultery is discovered, a momentary reconciliation takes place with Jane. (Appropriately the couple are reunited in scorn for Alicia's vulgar language, (94/82).) Jane acknowledges her need of Tom's body (99/86) and her good works extend to becoming 'good in bed'. Both Jane and Alicia are unbelievers. In contrast Marshfield's third lady, Frankie Harlow, is a professing Christian. Marshfield, however, still has trouble reconciling the body and the flesh. In Frankie's arms, unwilling to desecrate the spiritual, his organ fails to function altogether. Marshfield's attempts to establish erotic conjunction by the mediation of language also fail. Though he attempts to induce

Frankie to profess unbelief, coaching her word by word (155/133), the strategy founders upon her faith. Unable to reconcile body and spirit, Marshfield comes to see himself as desexualised by his religion: 'Ours is indeed a religion of women and slaves' (135/115). Taxed with his adultery by Frankie's husband, a banker whose 'stiff and manly palaver' (174/146), mixed with 'astronauts' lingo' appears to emanate from 'male mission control centre' (174/147), he senses that in pleading his innocence he had 'put on skirts in his eyes' (176/148). When a succession of female parishioners also seek counsel for their marital problems, Marshfield is able only to suggest that 'communication is often the real problem' (136/115).

Setting pen to paper in the motel Marshfield sets out to tackle that problem, which is very much the central focus of the novel. At first his writing reflects his previous failures in human connection. His first sentences are equated with onanism, in the image of 'sullying' blank sheets of paper (3/7), and he is successively voyeuristic and manipulative, converting his characters into things: 'dolls I can play with, putting them now in this, now in that obscene position' (178/150). Linguistic control falters however. In a multitude of typographic errors, Marshfield's unconscious surfaces through the control of language. 'Flash' becomes 'flesh' (14/16), his 'upraised' phallus becomes, sadly, 'unpraised' (34/32), 'kisses' turn into 'misses' (7/84), and Alicia's 'organ' into a threatening 'gorgan' (112/96). A funeral sermon is transformed into 'semon' (142/1421), conjoining sex and death, and 'impotent' becomes transmogrified into 'ompotent' (202/ 169), a quasi-omnipotence. Interestingly these errors were themselves serendipitous. Writing on an unfamiliar machine Updike made genuine typos, which he then incorporated into the text. 'I did more or less imitate [Marshfield's] "See what happens" attack.'[25] The impovisatory free-flowing style is repeatedly emphasised as Marshfield learns to allow language to slip and slide, with consequent gains in imaginative freedom and self-discovery. Lexical pranks, mock footnotes, puns, quotations, allusions, glosses, alliterative phrases, etymologies and games of word golf succeed each other in a prestidigitatory display of linguistic pyrotechnics. Marshfield's initial distate for the sloppy language of others (e.g. his sons' slang) is replaced by an equal dislike for formal precision. (He comments sarcastically on Ned and Jane's alternating stichomythia as converting them into a pair of hi-fi speakers (160/135).) The utterances of his senile father also demonstrate the power of the subconscious. Marshfield Senior dwells lubriciously on past sexual exploits, confusing his son with his brother, a companion in arms, a TV presenter and his wife's lover. Significantly Marshfield only manages to communicate with his father at all by entering his private fantasy (172/144). Marshfield's text continually evolves against his will. Tenses alternate ('Why can't I keep this in the present tense?' (28/28)) and he slips in and out of the first person. Defensively he presents one sequence (Alicia confronting Jane) as a scene from a soap opera. At another point he emphasises the arbitrary nature of his writing ('These sentences have come in no special order' (19/21)) only to recognise an unconscious patterning, in this case a correlation between his mother's sexuality and her singing voice. As the novel unfolds Marshfield's style becomes progressively less ornate and less of a means of shielding himself from meaningful interchange with others. In the last of his written sermons he reviews several examples of linguistic and literary inanity, ranging from singsong children's sermons to a work for Sunday School teachers and the gibberish of a 'cretinous prophecy' (207/172) proffered by a Jesus freak. Though sloppy and ill-expressed, Marshfield admits that even such flawed utterances bear witness to 'a miraculous raw truth' (208/173), and he questions:

Is not our distaste here aesthetic, where aesthetics are an infernal category. (208/173)

The comment occurs in one of four sermons, written on Sundays in the journal, in each of which Marshfield slowly accommodates to a less dualistic faith. In the first, on the woman taken in adultery, Christ is pictured writing idly and thus defeating the woman's accusers. The polemical apologetics for adultery is accompanied by a celebration of the power of writing. The second, on the miracles, attacks the ethical. Since disease continues, Christ's purpose in healing was not to accomplish good works but to demonstrate the existence of God. A third sermon on the desert and its denizens, signals a new acceptance of the physical world, while the fourth, which is actually addressed to his fellow motel-residents, concludes that 'our bodies are us' (209/

174). Each sermon is intentionally provocative, designed to dramatise Marshfield's emerging awareness that 'The Word is ever a scandal' (46/43),[26] that nothing is cut and dried or definable in dictionary terms. The surrounding stylistic context for the sermons erases the solidity of the text in similar fashion, dissolving the reader's certainties and undercutting the writer's control. The fidelity of Marshfield's account becomes as questionable as his marital fidelity, as he reinterprets, erases and rewrites, at one point even admitting that 'perhaps these words were never spoken. I made them up' (33/32). Even the title of the novel raises doubts, referring out to the proverbial month of Sundays which can never exist.

Marshfield anchors his own sense of identity to the existence of another person – the reader. In increasingly agonised terms, Marshfield ponders whether anyone is reading his pages, whether his 'Ideal Reader' exists. Only a reader can create his writing as a process of communication rather than a self-indulgent solipsism. Marshfield addresses the reader through a self-designated 'Ideal Reader', Ms Prynne, the motel manageress. This intertextual reference evokes the patron saint of American adultery, the heroine of Hawthorne's *The Scarlet Letter*, just as Jane Chillingworth recalls its villain, Roger Chillingworth, similarly indifferent to the needs of the body. In an essay on Hawthorne Updike has drawn attention to the former's 'instinctive tenet that matter and spirit are inevitably at war' (*Hugging the Shore*, p. 77). In the course of the novel, however, Marshfield sets out to overcome this dualism, intending his pages as a means to the seduction of Ms Prynne. After his final sermon Ms Prynne reveals her existence in a pencilled comment: 'Yes – at last, a sermon that could be preached'. (212/177). Marshfield then implores her to confirm his own existence: 'insofar as I exist on paper. Give me a body' (220/184). When Ms Prynne does finally give herself to him, on the morning of his departure, the last sentences of the novel record an erotic pairing in which each acknowledges the existence of the other. Ms Prynne's eyes are 'all for another' and Marshfield prays that his own face 'saluted in turn'. In a sense, by giving her body, Ms Prynne embodies Marshfield. In John T. Matthews's perceptive comment:

The novel's master conceit in many ways is that the book is the author's body, that the teleology of the act of writing is to join soul to body, a process compared in *A Month of Sundays* to the union of lovers.[27]

As the soul cannot exist without the body, so the book cannot exist without the reader. The process of writing thus becomes a process of self-analysis and understanding and a movement to reconciliation with others. Looking back on Frankie and Jane, Marshfield realises at last that his easy definitions were at fault. 'The one all ethics, the other all faith, and I between. No. The formulation does the reality a disservice' (203/170). At the close of the novel, therefore, responsibility for the text is passed from writer to reader. Narrative authority of an egotistical type is renounced in favour of an emphasis upon art as a two-way process of communication.

Not every reader will be seduced by *A Month of Sundays*. Indeed Updike's Ideal Reader would need to have a dictionary to hand to explicate unusual terms (boustrophedonic is one such) plus *Hastings Encyclopedia of Religion and Ethics* in order to appreciate the full range of theological puns. The novel none the less constitutes an indication of an important new direction in Updike's work. Quite minor themes in the novel (Vietnam, Feminism, the allocation of sex roles within Christianity) point forward to *The Witches of Eastwick*, in which Ed Parsley succeeds Marshfield's curate, Ned, as Jane Smart is a development of Alicia. Incidental references to the evils of technology and the expansion of the world's deserts touch upon a theme to be developed in *The Coup*. More importantly, the free-ranging, self-conscious, non-realist style of the novel presages later stylistic developments. Up to this point in his career Updike's works may be considered as broadly separable, into realistic social novels or flights into fantasy and aesthetic allegory. In *The Coup* and *The Witches of Eastwick*, as we shall see, the two streams conjoin in the service of a more overtly political art.

5

The Politics of the Imagination: *The Coup* and *The Witches of Eastwick*

As in *A Month of Sundays*, Colonel Ellelloû, the protagonist of *The Coup* is writing his memoirs, harnessing his memories to his imagination to recreate his own story and that of his country, Kush. As an imaginary African nation, newly emergent from colonialism and attempting to forge its identity amidst the warring claims of Marxism, Capitalism, Animism and Islam, Kush exists in an undefined territory, bordering on the realms of both the real and the fantastic. Considerable critical effort has been expended on the degree of correspondence between Kush and an African model.[28] Kathleen Lathrop has traced much of its politics, climate and topography to the country of Niger, with additional details drawn from other countries (Mali and Chad) which were until 1960 portions of French West Africa, noting that the drought which assails Kush is modelled upon the very real drought (from 1968) in the Sahel, a region which Updike visited in 1973. As Lathrop points out, much which may initially strike the reader as fantastic invention (e.g. the import of sorghum animal-feed for human consumption) is well-documented fact. Africa is, notoriously, a subject with thorns for the Western novelist. Other critics, notably Barry Amis and Joyce Markle, have read *The Coup* as an unmitigated fantasy, so riddled with inconsistencies and contradictions as to preclude any suspension of disbelief. Updike's own statement that the novel is in some respects an allegory of Watergate (the disgraced leader removed to restore his country's health) has further complicated the issue.[29] Although the novel constitutes a full-scale satiric attack on American materialism, consumerism and 'tricknology', in a sadly-familiar

115

tale of US neo-colonialism in the Third World, Africa's problems are too important in themselves merely to serve as the vehicle of Western dreams or nightmares. To read *The Coup* in conjunction with *The Witches of Eastwick*, however, suggests that Updike is explicitly addressing the question of the nature of the imagination in its relation to political power (a theme developed in the later novel). In both its imaginary location and in the unreliability of its narrator-protagonist, *The Coup* actively interrogates its own status as a work of the imagination, to form a highly self-conscious deliberation upon the parallel activities of fiction-making and of political exploitation.

In interview, Updike described his intention in the novel as the creation of 'a kind of echoing effect'.[30] For the alert reader acquainted with Updike's sources in African history, the echoes are manifold. Kush may not exist today but, to quote an eminent historian, 'the history of much of continental Africa is inseparable from the history of Kush'.[31] Located to the south of Egypt, conquered by the Egyptians and in turn conquering them (circa 751–716 B.C.), Kush was, at its zenith, a civilisation of extraordinary diversity and creative skill, trading far to the west from its capital at Meroë, until conquered and destroyed in its turn by the Axumites, under their king Ezana. Circumstantial evidence (which Updike exploits on 197/167, 226/191, 255/214) suggests that the royal house of Kush then fled westwards, perhaps even as far as Lake Chad. In selecting the name of Kush for the former Wanjiji-alias-Noire, the Revolutionary Council chooses to echo the earlier civilisation, much as other newly independent countries (e.g. Mali) have resurrected names which evoke past glories on behalf of national unity. In the light of Ellelloû's isolationism and hostility to technology, however, the name carries its own ironies. The historic Kush was the cradle of African technology, crucially important in the spread of iron-working. (Confronted with the mountains of slag around the ruins of Meroë, the archaeologist Sayce described it as the Birmingham of the Ancient World.) Ellelloû himself describes Kush as 'years removed from the original Kush, itself an echo: Africa held up a black mirror to Pharaonic Egypt, and the image was Kush' (4/10). Just as the country echoes and mirrors an earlier culture, itself reflecting Egyptian influence, so the names of Updike's characters also echo historical models. Ezana and Sheba (Ellelloû's fourth wife) need no introduction. Two other wives also recall Kushite queens. Candace is named for that legendary queen whose representative was converted by the Apostle Phillip (*Acts* VIII), while later queens of the province of Meroë held the title of Sittina (as James Bruce noted in 1772). Updike's purpose here, however is not merely to assist in the recuperation of African history. Other names evoke fictional echoes. Klipspringer, the US representative, steps into Kush from the pages of *The Great Gatsby*, while his Russian opposite number, Colonel Sirin, bears Nabokov's pen-name. In lending his characters the fluid outlines which correspond to a vexed identity, Updike invites speculation upon the connection between imaginative and political realities, situating the reader between fictional and historical models. Images of mirrors, masks, disguise and illusion reinforce the impression of an external space (Kush) onto which subjective realities are projected. The flag of Kush, a green field symbolising a vanished Saharan fertility, shimmers in the 'atmospheric mirrors of mirage' (33/33) above a parched colourless desert. The country itself, its outline drawn by white cartographers in the nineteenth-century scramble for Africa, enjoys little sense of nationhood, its northern borders nine-tenths imaginary, its peoples communicating with difficulty in 12 different languages, with the result that political events are echoed and distorted through a linguistic screen, to the point at which Kush exists quite variously in the different rhetorics of Animism, Islam, Marxism and Capitalism. If the national identity is elusive, that of its leader, a virtuoso quick-change artist, is even more so. Rarely photographed, Ellelloû figures at different points as a gum-seller, orange-peddlar, President, beggar, cook and insurance agent, under the titles of Colonel, Felix, Happy, Bini and Flapjack, among others. For the reader the novel thus overtly poses the question of African identity as an evolving self-construction. Readers blinkered by western images of Africa (e.g. as lacking a past) may write off as fantasy events which have a firm historical basis. Readers intent upon asserting an objective vision of African risk subjection to a Gradgrindian tyranny of fact at the expense of recognising that Africa has as much right to fantasy as to realism, to mythic ideals as to *realpolitik*. Updike, indeed, adroitly anticipates and undercuts one western reaction to his novel in the figure of Craven, Ellelloû's ex-professor. In Craven's view, Ellelloû's writing (an essay for a course in 'The Persistence of the Pharaonic Ideal in the Sudanic Kingdoms from 600–1600 A.D.')

is not sufficiently African: 'There was nothing strictly wrong, just my nebulous sense of something missing' (200/169). Ellelloû's response, 'Perhaps that is the very African ingredient,' is later borne out in the nebulous vacancies of Kush. Refusing to conform to Craven's 'idea of blackness' (202/171), Ellelloû asserts his right to his own imaginative powers: 'The realities of my people are not static, but in the process of transformation. Perhaps I can help create new realities' (200/170).

Within this general context of evolving realities, however, Ellelloû's imagination makes him an exceedingly unreliable narrator. Beginning his memoirs with a series of 'facts' culled from an outdated *Statesman's Year-Book*, Ellelloû goes on (as Markle has noted) to describe occurrences at which he was not present (the arrival of Angelica Gibbs, the escape of Ezana), eliding the temporal sequence, and obscuring his complicity in public decisions. The reader swiftly learns to read between the lines, translating Ellelloû's flights of rhetoric into objective reality ('The people of Kush reject capitalist intervention in all its guises' (40/39) i.e. the people of Kush are starving) and equally uncovering the individual horrors concealed beneath the tone of the objective reporter. (Ellelloû gains power 'upon the successful assassination attempt upon General Soba' (9/14), i.e. he had him killed. King Edumu's blind eyes remain 'sensitive to violent movement' (12/16), i.e. he has been tortured.) The disjunction between subjective and objective realities is also enacted in the narrative grammar of the novel in which Ellelloû alternates between first and third person, carefully separating his 'two selves; the one who acts, and the "I" who experiences' (7/12). This literary device provides Ellelloû with a handy means to evade his own responsibility for events. While his personal fiction of Kush is steadily starving its inhabitants to death, his imagination also assists him in the murder of individual victims, specifically Gibbs and Edumu.

Committed to an austere Islamic-Marxism, Ellelloû regards Western aid as not merely a palliative for the problems of Kush, but a materialist pollutant. When Donald Gibbs, a US Aid volunteer, confronts him with the realities of starvation and refers to Ellelloû's political writings, Ellelloû is infuriated: 'My privacy was invaded' (41/40). The invasion of his public space (Gibbs has imported supplies across the border) is secondary to his sense of personal violation. In his account of the death of Gibbs (burnt alive on a flaming pyramid of junk food) Ellelloû conceals his individual complicity by invoking an Islamic concept of fate. According to him, he gave a signal to the pyromaniac mob only 'so that the inevitable would appear to come from me' (42/41). Taxed with responsibility by King Edumu, however, he espouses Marxist determinism ('I am not the creator of this revolution but its instrument' (17/20)) and subsequently takes refuge from the facts of famine in readings from the Koranic celebration of Paradise.

Where Gibbs dies as a result of Ellelloû's Islamic-Marxist creed, King Edumu loses his head to the indigenous animist myth, that of the god-king ritually sacrificed to restore the fertility of the land, familiar to Western readers from the pages of *The Golden Bough* and *The Wasteland*. In executing Edumu, Ellelloû acts 'not as myself, not as Ellelloû, but as the breath of L'Emergence' (73/65), transposing a mythological structure of belief into revolutionary rhetoric. King Edumu sees through the deception to Ellelloû's conflicting allegiances:

> I say Kush is a fiction, an evil dream the white men had, and that [its rulers] are in truth white men, though their faces wear black masks. (69/63)

In addition to dramatising the murderous consequences of colliding imaginative myths, the execution scene also underlines the discrepancy between Ellelloû's solipsistic inner world, and external perspectives. On the scaffold, Ellelloû participates imaginatively in the king's experience, feeling 'his sensations, his struggling stiff frailty; I entered in, was pushed and pulled among jostling selves of muscular darkness' (73/66). Imaginative projection, however, is speedily followed by the descent of the scimitar, cleaving a path through the air like 'a long flaw in crystal' (73/66). While Ellelloû refracts the event through the reflective mirrors of his own subjective rhetoric, it appears quite differently to the outside world. From the distant vantage point of the crowd, the affair is one of tiny puppets (75/76). Only a few onlookers can understand the King's speech (in Wanj) and when Tuaregs make off with his head many spectators assume that this 'kaputnapping' is also part of the spectacle. Whether within or without, comprehension is strictly limited by the constricting ideological and individual frames within which the execution is viewed.

Where the opening sequences of the novel reveal the potential murderousness of the imagination in relation to political events, Chapters 4 to 6 focus upon the hero's personal existence. Assuming the mantle of Grail-knight, intent on restoring the rains, Ellelloû sets off on a quasi-pilgrimage across the inhospitable Balak in search of the King's head in its Chapel Perilous, a mountain cave. Appropriately he is accompanied in this martyrdom of the flesh by his fourth wife, Sheba, an ethereal beauty whose 'gentle spirit rarely descended to earth' (145/125), largely as a result of her continuous ingestion of hallucinogenic substances. The entire sequence insists upon the vacancy of the external scene, and the resultant primacy of an internal world. The Balak, travelled largely in darkness, becomes as immaterial as fiction, its fine, black and white sand 'an immense page of print too tiny to read' (131/113), its colourlessness lending Sheba's beauty 'a blueprint precision' (129/112), her features emphasised 'as if by an ink-laden fine quill' (129/112). Even the caravan to which the pair are attached carries a contraband load of typewriter components, erasers, ribbons and pens. In the desert Ellelloû recalls an argument with black activists in America about the necessity for myth. For Ellelloû 'the truth of a mythology should not be judged evidentially piece by piece but by its *gestalt* result' (139/120). What matters to him is not objective fact but the potential sustaining power of a subjective fiction: 'the crucial question isn't Can you prove it? but does it give us a handle on the reality that otherwise would overwhelm us?' (141/121). Ironically, thirsty and starving in the Balak, Ellelloû sustains himself not on the Grail myth, but on the American dream, his actual experiences in the desert alternating with vividly recreated memories of Wisconsin. On one level these memories reveal that Ellelloû's political vision of Kush is a reflection-in-reverse, a negative print of America, his austerity a reaction to American plenty, and his Islam derived from American Black Muslims, from whose ideas he has constructed a syncretic concept of Kush: 'Crystals of dreaming erected within me, and the nation of Kush as it exists is the residue of those crystals' (161/138). As in America he imagined Kush, so in Kush he imagines America. Reviewing his love-affair with Candace, Ellelloû also recognises the personal consequences of his existence between two worlds, neither of which is entirely real. Where Candace's America has struck him as an 'elaborate trap' (151/129), he is attracted to Sheba as 'vacancy'. In contrast to Candace's jealous possessiveness, Sheba is undemanding;

> Where another woman had an interior, a political space that sent its emissaries out to bargain for her body and her honour, Sheba had a space that asked no tending, that supported a nomadic traffic of music and drugs.   (148/127)

In her self-immersion and isolation from reality, Sheba exists in parallel with Ellelloû's dream of Kush. Just as she goes forward on a mixture of kola, bhang and khat, so Ellelloû sustains himself on flickering memories of an America which no longer exists, as unreal as 'bits of a Fifties movie, with its studiously recruited cross-section meant to emblemize the melting-pot, the fertile and level prairie of American goodness' (136/117). As death menaces, Ellelloû recognises that his trek with Sheba is a reenactment of both his erotic history and his political romance of leadership:

> I thought of all the women I had led into such a wilderness, a promised green land of love that then had turned infertile, beneath the mono-maniacal eye of my ambition, my wish to create a nation, to create a nation as a pedestal for myself, my pathetic self.   (183/156)

In ensuing developments the *gestalt* result of Ellelloû's faith in contradictory mythologies becomes all too evident. Paradoxically, in his hostility to technology and materialism, he has played into the hands of the technocrats and pragmatists. While he has been pursuing a myth across the desert, Ezana has quietly consolidated his power, until events culminate in a bloodless coup and an influx of Western advisers. At the end of the trek, Ellelloû loses Sheba, whose fate (carried off to slavery in a Yemeni air-conditioned kitchenette) symbolises the neo-colonial enslavement of Kush. The pilgrimage itself ends in the narrow confines of the cave in which the Russians, profiting from Ellelloû's animist myth, have installed the King's head as a tourist attraction and propaganda vehicle. 'Courtesy of Soviet technology' (214/180) the head is restored to life, wired for sound

and displayed against the background of a slide show. A recorded
message denounces Ellelloû:

> He has projected upon the artificial nation of Kush his own
> furious though ambivalent will; the citizens of this poor nation
> are prisoners of his imagination.   (212/180)

As Ellelloû grapples with the head the tables are turned upon him
in no uncertain terms. Fragments of the slideshow of the Kush
national heritage flicker across his back, so that for once he
actually embodies Kush, but a Kush of fantasy, its images
projected upon his own blankness. Importantly, he remains
completely unrecognised by the spectators, until the naked power
of his henchmen's guns restores his identity and authority.

Unfortunately, that identity coincides in name with a booming
oil town, christened for Ellelloû, which exhibits all the features of
that image of small town America which sustained him in the
desert. Ellelloû thus ends up, back in the movie of his past,
surrounded by Fifties records, hamburger joints and upwardly
mobile workers. When he makes one last effort to rally the citizens
of Kush against Western materialism, he finds himself dependent
upon the technology he decries. Although he feels momentarily
potent, holding the microphone of a public address system 'as if he
had seized a gun' (249/209), his rhetoric is at the mercy of external
power supplies. When the current is cut off, a mob intent on free
beer stampede over their President. Where previously Ellelloû
had invoked myth, he now becomes its victim. As he falls, a little
cloud covers the sun, presaging the monsoon rains which, he
recognises, 'I achieved by ceasing to exist. *I* was the curse upon
the land' (261/219). With his fall from power, Ellelloû's identity is
engulfed by myth. In the public history of Kush every political
event has ostensibly been carried forward in his name, including
the crushing of the French, and the revolution, all now converted
into one long triumphant sequence dependent upon 'the grand
ellisions of historical myth' (261/219). Kush has finally rewarded
him with mythical status, in order to remove an impediment to
materialist evolution. As Kutunda informs Ellelloû: 'The time for
fables is over for Africa. We must live among stern realities'
(284/238).

The novel does not close, however, on such an unambiguous
rejection of imagined worlds. If the imagination fosters non-

existent and pernicious visions, so remote from reality as to engender a dangerous power-vacuum, it also creates necessary dreams. Just as, during the drought, Ellellou, masquerading as an orange-seller, sustains his people with a song purveying the image of oranges (77/68), so he eventually gains a pension in exile for a song. Ezana, who has no desire to lead but favours a snug existence as bureaucratic *éminence grise*, acknowledges that, for his *realpolitik* to function, he needs paper gods, symbolic leaders to appeal to the imagination of the people. Previously he had recognised that 'He and Ellellou needed one another as the earth needs the sky' (170/145). Between them a synthesis had emerged, with Kush 'born of the dialectical space between us' (117/101). As this synthesis collapses, Ezana is quick to fill the gap with President Dorfû, whose name, erroneously translated as 'solidarity', symbolises material glut in its real meaning: 'torpor suffered by a reptile when it has swallowed too big a meal' (282/236). Uneasily aware that, as an unimaginative materialist, he cannot long command the allegience of Kush, Dorfû sets Ellellou free: 'On a continent where materialism has yet to cast its full spell, a live man far away is less of a presence than a dead man underfoot' (289/242)

For all his solipsism, Ellellou's defeat at the hands of a crudely materialist ideology carries its own pathos. On returning to Istiqlal, Ellellou visits the home of his first wife, Kadongolimi. Earler in the novel, Kadongolimi had reminisced about the life of the village in which they both grew up, celebrating its arts, creativity and pervasive spirituality:

> The gods gave life to every shadow, every leaf. Everywhere we looked there was spirit. At every turn of our lives, spirit greeted us. We knew how to dance, awake or asleep. No misery could touch the music in us. Let other men die in chains; we lived. (95/84)

Ageing and obese, however, Kadongolimi's spirit sinks beneath the weight of her flesh; she dies, her heart smothered, crying out for space (273/228). Where Sheba represented a fantasy Africa, Candace the American dream, Kadongolimi is the 'earth-strength' (92/81) of indigenous belief, combining flesh, spirit and imagination in a synthesis now in collapse. At the close of the novel Ellellou goes into exile with his third wife, Sittina,

Westernised, but persistently in motion, a wind of change incarnate. Significantly, Sittina is also an artist, though none of her works are completed. Because 'There's something so dead about a finished painting' (296/248), Sittina intentionally leaves blank corners, unfilled outlines and empty spaces. In Sittina's landscapes that 'nebulous sense of something missing' is left as a free space for the imagination. Updike's novel, moving between the frontiers of the real and the imaginary to create its own half-echoes and obscure reflections, provides the reader with a similar space. Like Jerry and Ruth Conant, Ellelloû and Sittina relocate themselves in France, where 'Africa has been . . . legitimized by art' (297/248). As in *Marry Me*, however, Updike is swift to undercut any notion of finality. At the end of the novel the solidity of Ellelloû's memoirs is erased, in a disclaimer which insists upon their incompleteness.

> He is writing his memoirs. No, I should put it more precisely: Colonel Ellelloû is rumored to be working on his memoirs. (299/250)

Ellelloû's imaginative creations are therefore delegitimised in the resumption of the suspect third-person voice. In its interplay of fictions, myths and countermyths, *The Coup* undercuts the powers of the imagination as it celebrates them, only to deconstruct itself in its turn. Updike's syncretic Africa, a melange of fact and invention, myth and reality, provides a location in which to explore the warring claims of matter and spirit, public abstraction and private fantasy, within a political context. In *The Witches of Eastwick* that context is brought closer to home as Updike extends his discussion of the role of technology, power and the imagination, in relation to the America of the Vietnam years.

In 1978 John Updike reviewed a reissue of Sylvia Townsend Warner's *Lolly Willowes* (1962). In Warner's novel a middle-class English lady politely declines marriage and settles instead for becoming a witch, abandoning family life for a village in Buckinghamshire where she acquires a 'familiar', joins a coven and makes a pact with Satan. As Updike notes in his review, the witch is identified here with nature, and is presented as a positive image of the liberated woman. When Updike recommended the novel to a feminist friend, 'she scowled and said, "Of course that's what men like to tell us. Either marry one of them or become a witch."' Updike concluded, 'Let us respectfully construe the word "witch" as "free woman"' (*Hugging the Shore*, p. 306). To readers brought up on the conical-hatted crones of Walt Disney, the suggestion may seem startling, but the witches of *The Witches of Eastwick* have as much in common with *Lolly Willowes* as with Halloween. Although a novel about practising witches in contemporary Rhode Island may appear as fantastic as a novel about a centaur in Pennsylvania, *The Witches of Eastwick* needs to be understood against a solidly documented social background. In the novel Updike examines a modern synthesis of beliefs, drawn from different sources but mutually coherent and interconnective. Feminism, radical theology and ecological issues are drawn together by the figure of the witch, which also has a special significance in relation to the war in Vietnam.

Writings on modern witchcraft are both voluminous in quantity and of extremely diverse intellectual quality. What emerges, however, is that modern America has been marked by an immense resurgence of interest in witchcraft.[32] On 25 May 1978, Jack Anderson reported in a syndicated column that the US Army had taken steps to ensure that its chaplains would be willing and able to minister to the increasing number of military personnel who declared themselves to be witches. Jeffrey B. Russell[33] reports some 10,000 self-styled witches in America, with whole journals devoted to the cult and a booming commerce in the occult. While America has never been a stranger to bizarre cults and esoteric forms of the sacred, in some areas witchcraft is fast approaching the status of a religion. Individual covens vary in their precise beliefs and are eclectic in their rituals, but may generally be characterised as taking one of two forms: neo-paganism or Satanism. Much of Updike's novel will become intelligible in the light of the neo-paganist synthesis.

Contemporary neo-paganism has its roots in the 1920s when Margaret Murray published *The Witch Cult in Western Europe*[34] from which Updike draws many incidental details for his novel. In Murray's thesis historical witchcraft was a survival of a widespread and ancient fertility religion, involving the worship of a horned god and earth goddess, covens, witches' sabbaths and ritual observances. Murray's work was immensely influential (she wrote the entry on witchcraft for the *Encyclopaedia Britannica* from 1929 to 1968) though her grasp of historical method was almost nonexistent and her findings were largely discredited when

Norman Cohn[35] discovered that she had edited her sources to make her case. Interest was further revived after World War II in Britain, under the aegis of Gerald Gardner, who claimed to have been initiated into the cult by a surviving witch, and who placed more emphasis on the Goddess than on the Horned God. Today more sophisticated witches have abandoned Gardner's claims for the cult as an ancient traditional religion, arguing in favour of its validity in terms of poetic, spiritual and psychological creativity. The pre-eminence of the goddess in modern covens has also made them attractive to some feminists. When, in 1968, WITCH, the Women's International Terrorist Conspiracy from Hell was founded as a political pressure group (the acronym was a joke) its members were surprised to find that they were approached by practising witches. Although most feminists see witchcraft as a foolish diversion from political goals, others have been attracted to its female orientation. Mary Daley, a radical theologian, has expressed sympathy for a goddess-centred religion. Naomi Goldenberg, in particular, has studied neo-paganist witchcraft which she situates in the context of reaction to patriarchal Christianity, and to the marginal place assigned to women within it.[36] Two points relevant to Updike's novel emerge from Goldenberg's analysis: the psychological inner-direction of witchcraft, and the connection between its beliefs and larger political issues.

Modern witchcraft has a strong psychological cast to it. Modern witches see the goddess as an internal presence in the worshipper, almost a Muse, inspiring the female members of the coven to creative work. Essentially a theistic religion, witchcraft conceives of its deity as a set of internal images and attitudes. Any thought or fantasy is considered real in so far as it has power to influence actions in the present. (A remembered fact or an invented fantasy therefore have identical psychological power.) Since witches believe that thoughts and actions form around psychological imagery, they therefore feel that a woman will be a more effective feminist if her deep imaginal life has a feminist tone as well as her everyday political life. Most witch-magic and ritual is designed to stimulate the imagination and to foster individual strengths. Covens are non-hierarchical and each member is a goddess in the sense of being potentially divine in power. Witches are encouraged to focus their wills, often by the use of a mirror to contemplate the self-as-goddess, or by such group activities as 'raising the cone of power', the combined will of the group, intensified through ritual techniques and focused on an end collectively agreed upon. Women's autonomy is fostered and supported by an overall emphasis on individual creativity and expression, openness to nature and the unconscious, and the importance of the female principle. Erica Jong's recent *Witches*,[37] which sees historical witch-hunting as a means to the political repression of women, includes poems, paintings, prose and pencil drawings all designed to demonstrate what the figure of the witch can teach women about their inner selves. As far as magical practices are concerned, modern neo-pagans apparently abjure any form of *maleficium* (magic designed to harm), essentially holding that to work magic is to be in touch with the energy flow of the cosmos, moving with it and shaping it gently to one's ends.

In political terms the emphasis on nature as sacred means that the movement is strongly ecological and understands itself as distinguished from Judaeo-Christian tradition in this respect. Witches argue that Christianity sells women a male god and therefore denies them the experience of seeing themselves as divine or powerful. Angered by Judaeo-Christian traditions which appear to denigrate the body of woman (specifically in Christ's antiseptic conception) and to polarise woman into passive asexual virgin and wicked witch, cult members see their dominant culture as worshipping an abstracted god of death, debasing women and nature together. Witches are not of course the only ones to have drawn a connection between religious tradition and disrespect for nature. Cultural historians have also posited a link between the abandonment of female earth-religions in favour of a male sun-god, Christian or otherwise, and the emergent creed of technological and capitalist growth. Various religious thinkers have argued that the ecology crisis has been engendered by a Judaeo-Christian derogatory attitude to non-human life[38] and by the belief that it is man's destiny to conquer nature and harness *her* for *his* ends. Brian Easlea has argued that scientific and technological appropriation of the earth constitutes a display of male virility.[39] Scientists can control nature and revel in the joy of conquest, leading to the triumph of what Lewis Mumford has called 'the myth of the machine'.[40] In Mumford's historical analysis, the triumph of the sky religions is accompanied by a new emphasis on the orderly, the calculable, the controlled and the clean, with predictable consequences in

terms of political absolutism and regimentation. The idea has
been extended in recent discussions of relationships between the
sexes. Oldenberg refers particularly to the work of Dorothy
Dinnerstein,[41] which interestingly emphasises the collaboration
of women with the technological myth. Dinnerstein argues that,
because child care is primarily assigned to women, both sexes
grow up to identify woman with raw nature, the primal resource,
and men with cleanliness, order and control. In her view we all
want men to control women and nature so that our infant
experience of being vulnerable to women's power will not be
repeated. The results of this cultural assignation of sex roles may
be seen in our attitudes to military and technological activities.
Because women can 'bring out the baby' in men, reminding them
of their early dependence, men evolve sex-segregated activities as
a sanctuary from women. War is an obvious example. In common
with other 'countercultural' systems of belief, modern witchcraft
rejects body/soul dualism, together with public political
hierarchies, and emphasises the cyclic nature of time, rather than
the linear progessive model. As a result the cult valorises the inner
life (subjectivity, imagination, feeling) in opposition to science,
logic or objectivity, with a concomitant belief in the power of
consciousness to control history. This belief that a revolution in
consciousness will resolve the world's problems was
demonstrated when, on 1 August 1971, a number of Californian
covens joined together in a concerted ritual attempt to end the
war in Vietnam.

Individual readers may or may not find the preceding analysis
convincing or congenial to their own beliefs. The fact remains that
neo-paganism appears to be relatively life-enhancing and has
attracted serious attention. The darker side to this resurgence of
interest is clearly visible, however, in the renewal of Satanism in
America. Modern Americans are bombarded with Satanic
imagery, from horror-movies, popular press accounts of 'ritual
slayings', Hell's Angels, the Manson family murders, and a
plethora of pulp novels. Like neo-paganist witchcraft, Satanism is
openly practised in America. In 1966 Anton Szander la Vey
founded the First Church of Satan in San Francisco (listed in the
San Francisco telephone directory under 'Churches: Satanist'),
attracted a congregation of 7000 people and published *The Satanic
Bible* (1969). La Vey (real name Howard Levy) appears to be a
comic figure, well aware of his own showmanship. Formerly a

lion-tamer, a calliope player in a circus, a nightclub entertainer, police photographer and palm reader, he dedicated *The Satanic Bible* to Phineas T. Barnum, among others. In his 'Foreword' to *Soundings in Satanism* Updike, however, took issue with the contemporary tendency to view the devil as comic, voicing the minority view ironically:

> Can evil be a personal, dynamic, principle? The suggestion seems clownish, instinctively we reject it. If we must have a supernatural, at the price of intellectual scandal, at least let it be a minimal supernatural, clean, monotonous, hygienic, featureless. (*Picked-Up Pieces*, p. 87)

In Updike's view Americans diminish God to the creation of their own imaginations (the leap of faith), reducing the devil to 'the dimensions of a bad comic strip'. In the remainder of his 'Foreword' Updike ponders the question: Is evil the product of technology or of nature? His comments suggest that he has absorbed the terms of the current debate. On the one hand the temptation to do evil may be understood as a reaction against a technologised, orderly existence:

> the more completely order would enclose us, the greater the threat to our precious creaturely freedom, which finds self-assertion in defiance and existence in sin and dreads beyond hell a heaven of automatons . . . our own supertechnology breeds witches and warlocks from the loins of engineers. (*Picked-Up Pieces*, p. 90)

On the other hand Updike notes that man is naturally beset by disease, predators, parasites, floods and earthquakes, suggesting that nature is at best indifferent to man, and that modern technology may therefore be on the side of the angels:

> The Christian West with its myth of the devil, has taken the fight to Nature with a vengeance, has sought out the microbe and dammed the river and poisoned the mosquito in his marsh, and gouged the mineral from its hidden vein and invented the machines that now threaten to scrape Nature into the infernal abyss. (*Picked-Up Pieces*, p. 90)

As the last phrase implies, Updike remains undecided here as to whether technology represents a force for good or a second form of cooperation with evil. In *The Witches of Eastwick*, plot, imagery and narrative structure are designed to explore the relation between technology, sexual relations, nature and religious beliefs. Updike sets three neo-paganist witches and a comic buffoon of a devil against a background of expanding technological and military activity. The novel is set in the last year of the Vietnam war to which a series of allusions is made. Structurally the novel continually opposes inner subjective experience to the public activities of the outer world, while image patterns of decay, disease and waste are contrasted with imagery of cleanliness, order and control. Although Updike's own Christian faith is a matter of record and not of debate, the novel actively re-assesses the contribution of religious beliefs to technological expansion.

In the initial section of the novel, 'The Coven', Updike's portrayal of the three witches, Alexandra, Sukie and Jane, emphasises the neo-paganist, feminist synthesis, setting his characters in a representative locale. Eastwick is a centre for the new 'clean' technology. In the former cornfields stand windowless plants with names like Dataprobe and Computech, manufacturing components so fine that employees wear plastic caps to keep dandruff out of the works. While the area has been vandalised by technology, its beaches littered with non-degradable garbage, its fields now asphalted shopping malls and parking lots, it also contains unexplored areas of natural beauty and marshes where egrets nest. Its salt atmosphere attacks metal, and is described as an air which 'empowered women' (8). Alexandra's tomatoes, Sukie's zucchini, are preposterously fertile. Casting off male dominance, along with their technological husbands, the three women have gained new powers. Alexandra's former husband, Ozzie, a maker of chrome bathroom fixtures (cleanliness and technology) has undergone a representative evolution, dwindling:

> first to the size of a mere man, the armour of protector falling from him in the corrosive salt air of Eastwick's maternal beauty, and then to the size of a child as his chronic needs and equally chronic acceptance of her solutions to them made him appear pitiful and manipulable. (7)

Where Sukie's husband, Monty, took refuge from 'uppity' women in golf, Ozzie involves himself in his sons' Little League activities, and in his company's all-male bowling team. All three women are divorced, and have magically reduced their husbands to dust (Ozzie), a permanised place mat (Monty) and a dried herb (Sam Smart). At this stage of the novel witchcraft appears as a simple affirmation of female freedom, on a level with Alexandra's adoption of comfortable unfashionable clothes and her impatience with male-oriented definitions of bodily beauty. Alexandra expands physically with her powers and her tomato sauce, refusing to deny the body in the belief that nature is the index of health and bodily appetites exist to be satisfied. Raising a storm to clear the beach, Alexandra describes her powers as the result of the 'reappropriation of her assigned self', easily achieved once 'power had been assigned to the primary pole, oneself as a woman' (15). Emanicipation from male control has also given each witch a renewed creativity. Alexandra creates clay 'bubbies', small primal images of earthy, sexual women, Jane plays the cello, and Sukie writes, if only social tittle-tattle for the Eastwick *Word*. Raising the cone of power at their Thursday covens, the witches function as a sisterly support group, engaging in mutual confidence-building. Jane and Sukie jolly Alexandra out of her ever-present fear of cancer, represented here as a result of the loss of psychic faith in nature. Sukie and Alexandra encourage Jane to cultivate her musical talents, in terms which dissociate them from contemporary military rhetoric: ' "She wastes herself," Alexandra said. . . . "Wastes in the old-fashioned sense," she added, since this was during the Vietnam War and the war had given the word an awkward new meaning' (26). Such malice as their meetings involve is of a jokey, gossippy nature, and the magic which they practise appears to take place on the level of the practical joke (breaking a string of beads, snapping a watch strap, untying shoe laces) with comic results and no real harm done.

This feminist haven, however, does not remain one for long. Darryl Van Horne's first entrance estasblishes his diabolical nature. Dark, hairy, horny, with odd, pointy shoes and a name of obvious symbolic significance, Van Horne is a technologist intent on exploiting synthetic polymers and the interface between solar and electrical energy. He concludes a brief scientific lecture with:

the beauty of it is, you can grow the raw materials and when you

run out of land you can grow 'em in the ocean. Move over,
Mother Nature, we've got you beat.   (47)

In his first conversation with Ed Parsley, liberal anti-war pastor,
Van Horne lays his cards on the table. The two men clash
aggressively over the connection between the war and the
commerce and technology of Eastwick, with Van Horne firmly on
the side of Mammon. Renovating the Lenox mansion, Van Horne
cheerfully fills in the wetlands, displacing the snowy egrets in
favour of an artificial tennis court and an immense hot-tub,
expensive stereophonic equipment, and an investment collection
of works of art (vinyl hamburgers, Brillo cartons, a woman
constructed of chicken wire and beer cans) which essentially
represent the permanized garbage of a consumer society. The
town, eager for Van Horne's taxes, reacts enthusiastically. As the
Word jauntily reports, 'Progress has its price!' (65)
   Yet for all their distaste the witches speedily come under Van
Horne's spell. The first signs of sisterly disunity appear as they vie
for his attention and abandon their Thursday meetings. Van
Horne's attraction depends upon the inherent weakness of the
witches' set of ideas. In the first place the witches fail to take him
seriously. He appears a comically clumsy figure, shambling,
bearish, poorly coordinated and spitting when he talks.
Alexandra looks back and remembers 'the amiable human
awkwardness of it all' (121). The women are committed to a view
of sexual relations which infantilises men, separating the sexes
into woman the powerful nurturing figure, man the helpless
dependant. Their other sexual relationships reinforce the point.
Sukie sees herself as 'mothering' (77) her boss, Clyde. Jane's
relationship with passive Raymond Neff and Sukie's with the
imploring Ed Parsley both figure as healing relationships in which
the women consider their bodies as a means 'to apply the poultice
of acquiescent flesh to the wound of a man's desire' (69). In
consequence, Alexandra sees Van Horne as merely 'a bundle of
needs' (49). Darryl is swift to exploit the women's prejudices. He
dwells on his youthful adoration of his mother and his resentment
of his 'wimp' of a father (113). He applauds women's lack of
squeamishness in relation to the body. In a cunning echo of a
respectable feminist thesis[42] he describes the origin of the
historical witch-craze as an attempt to take midwifery out of the
hands of women, with a subsequent rise in fatalities as male

doctors worked beneath sheets obscuring the body. In addition Van Horne, for all his technology, successfully appeals to the women's instincts for defiance of order. When Alexandra is trapped by the rising tide in the Lenox mansion, she thinks she has made good her escape by divesting herself of her clothes and wading the creek. The terms of her response, however, suggest a deeper entrapment. She laughs at her own folly in getting stranded: 'The spirit needs folly as the body needs food' (99). Echoing Updike's analysis of the attractions of folly, Alexandra concludes that:

> A natural principle was being demonstrated, that of divestment. We must lighten ourselves to survive. . . . Only folly dares those leaps that give life. This dark man on his island was possibility. (101)

Divesting themselves entirely on Halloween in Van Horne's hot tub, the witches yield to Darryl's dominance on the grounds that his system of exchange 'at least dealt in assets – bodies, personal liveliness – they did have and not in spiritual goods laid up in some nonexistent Heaven' (122). Yet for all the fleshly joys of the heated pit with its stereophonic harmonies and sliding roof revealing the stars, the final lines of 'The Coven' strike a jarring note. The unnamed narrator of the novel makes an equation between the witches' doings and the war. Gossip is spreading about them, for in Eastwick 'as in Washington and Saigon there were leaks' (121). Emerging from the house, Alexandra feels completely clean, her flesh rarefied by its immersion in the tub, as if she were yielding to the clean, anti-flesh joys of technology. Glancing up through her tinted windshield at the moon, she imagines for a second that

> astronauts had landed and in an act of imperial atrocity had spray-painted that vast sere surface green. (123)

Under the guise of celebrating nature and disorder, Van Horne has trapped the witches within the technological myth of the machine, masking his conquest with sensual delights and a rhetoric which exploits the arguments of the feminist synthesis.

In the second section of the novel, 'Malefica', however, this apparent opposition between technological evil and female good is revealed as an oversimplification of the complex issues at stake.

Ostensibly 'good' figures are revealed in the full confusion of their motives. Two representatives of the counterculture figure significantly. Ed Parsley, introduced as an opponent of the war, elopes with Dawn Polanski, also a war-protester, to join the Movement. While Ed looks like an embodiment of enlightened Christianity, he is actually motivated by the desire not to appear ineffectual and soft. As his initial clash with Darryl demonstrates, Ed wishes to assert his own virility. In an ironic allusion to Mumford's *The Pentagon of Power* Sukie comments that 'He wanted power. A woman can give a man power over himself in a way, but she can't put him in the Pentagon' (134). Ed was attracted to the counterculture as 'another System, equally fierce and far flung' (43) as its opposite, and joins it rather as if he were joining the army. Ironically he is blown up by one of the bombs he was making in an effort to restore world peace. The episode suggests that simple opposition to the system on its own terms merely replaces one militarist evil with another.

More important, however is the account of Clyde Gabriel's murder of his wife Felicia and subsequent suicide. Initially Felicia appears as an affirmative figure, embodying pacifist and ecological virtue. A keen member of the Wetlands Watchdog Committee and an equally fervent campaigner against the war, Felicia tells Clyde that the world is not a tidy diagram but an organism, vital and sensitive. Clyde, a caricature of Mumford's cosmological technocrat, takes refuge from her in the pages of *Scientific American*. Years before, Clyde had written a paper on 'The Supposed Conflict Between Science and Religion', concluding that there was none, but now he realises that the conflict is implacable and science is winning. Clyde's favourite authors are those he characterises as the great seers through – Nietzsche, Hume, Gibbon. He enjoys stargazing, and has a taste for terrestrial disasters, floods, earthquakes and volcanic eruptions. It might appear that, as a classically anti-feminist villain, Clyde kills Felicia because she talks too much. The precise description of the murder invites a more subtle reading. Sukie and Jane have 'hexed' Felicia so that as she talks she continually spits out slimy foul-tasting waste. In her righteous indignation, her eyes burn 'like the tiny flames of votive candles' (153) and her hair stands up in a ragged halo. Faced with these conflicting images of woman-as-saint, woman-as-filth, Clyde resolves the contradiction by force. He concludes that Felicia is possessed, and smashes her head with a poker, 'Just to interrupt the flow of energy for a moment, to plug the hole through which too much was pouring' (153). Imagistically the description suggests an outpouring of sexual aggression. More specifically, the murder draws on Mumford's thesis. Mumford notes that the 'rise of civilisation' (the political unification of the Upper and Lower Nile valley, and the triumph of male cosmological religions centred upon a Sun-god) was accompanied by wholesale slaughter. Mass graves from the period reveal quantities of smashed skulls.[43] In the same connection Mumford refers to the Babylonian epic in which Marduk's struggle with the primeval goddess Tiamat ends in triumph when he smashes her skull with his mace.

Clyde's reaction to the murder reinforces the preceding suggestions. As a child Clyde had loved neatness and cleanliness, and had been fascinated by the orderly lines of architectural drawings. He had been particularly drawn to those with a precise vanishing point, confirming his belief in a calculable universe without mysteries. After the murder Clyde feels restored to a world of clarity, as in the illustrations to his favourite children's books. Complications are swept away, 'leaving the outlines of this room, the lines of its carpentry clean as laser beams' (155). He compares himself to a clean suit emerging from its wrappings, rejects various alternative methods of suicide as messy (157) and selects from the laundry room a clothesline with which to hang himself. Clyde's last moments pass in careful observation of the architecture of his house, and in methodical calculation of the length of the rope, the depth of the drop, and the mechanics of death. He chooses to die, appropriately, in front of the symmetrical sunrise of his fanlight.

Despite the quality of caricature inherent in Clyde, Updike generates some sympathy for his plight. When Clyde dies, his calculations have failed to prepare him for his wildly swinging motion and for the burning in his throat. Felicia is no innocent victim either. Like Ed, Felicia has been motivated by abstract concerns. When the town wishes to rename Landing Square after Kazmierczak, their former quarterback, killed in Vietnam, Felicia pours scorn on the suggestion and gloats over the young man's death. While having a considerable love of the unprivileged in theory, actual cases repel her. Roused in anger, Felicia is described as employing a polished rhetoric, aimed at an imaginary crowd, 'troops she was leading' (152). The witches' own reactions to the death also foreground the war. Both Sukie and Jane have now adopted current rhetoric. Sukie describes Clyde as having 'wasted' Felicia's head, and Jane adds that he then 'wasted' himself (162). Sukie is confirmed in her belief in the subjective control of reality, maintaining that her hex killed Felicia. When Jane disagrees, 'Words are just words' (165), Sukie counters that words 'make things happen'. Importantly, during the last night she spent with Clyde, Sukie had 'mothered' him in the sexual act, remaining unsatisfied herself until a dream image of Felicia completed her orgasm. For the witches, internal, female images are of prime significance. Jane writes off Felicia's murder as the logical result of her loss of contact with her womanhood (165). When Brenda Parsley attempts to draw a moral, the witches are dismissive. Brenda, Alexandra reports:

> tried to make some connection between their deaths and Vietnam, the moral confusion of the times. I didn't quite follow it. (169)

For the informed reader, not only is the connection more obvious, but the witches' reactions also confirm their solipsistic immersion in a subjective world.

Where Ed, Clyde and Felicia appear to be caught in the contradictions of 'the myth of the machine', and have sacrificed their inner lives to abstract or world-wide concerns, the witches have gone to the other extreme. The Gabriels' deaths introduce two new characters into the novel, their children Chris and Jenny, whose appearance polarises the coven into male and female groups. Initially the witches see themselves as mothering Jenny, a radiography technician, bombarded by X-rays and therefore apparently a victim of the machine. Sukie sees Jenny as 'an undernurtured waif' (172) and promptly uses her magical powers to feed her thick cream. The trio set to work to thaw out their little ice maiden in Darryl's tub, massaging, oiling and worshipping the body. They respond to Jenny, less as a real child, than as a version of each woman's younger self (215). Significantly they enjoy the sight of her reduced image in the diminishing perspective of the poolroom mirrors. Their nurturing is revealed as an illusion. The childishness of Clyde's tidy world exists in counterpoint to the witches' equally immature subjective disorder. As the sessions develop, the witches regress to a state of dependence in which

Jenny serves them, Sukie reverts to thumbsucking, and their voices become babyish and undifferentiated. 'In Van Horne's realm they left their children behind and became children themselves' (213). The narrator characterises them as part of a general malaise, which includes the teenagers in front of the Superette, waiting for their weekly dope delivery, the drunkard seeking oblivion in Kazmericzak Square, and the adulterers getting their fix of motel love:

> all sacrificing the outer world to the inner, proclaiming with this priority that everything solid-seeming and substantial is in fact a dream, of less account than a merciful rush of feeling.   (207)

The unreality of their subjective heaven is pointedly indicated in the tennis match which the four women organise. Sealed into an artificial environment, enclosed beneath the court's inflated dome, the women play in a heated warmth distinct from the outer chill of the shortest day of the year. Unlike their previous jokey games, this match becomes a furious competition, a war in which their magic is used for harm, converting the ball into a series of offensive missiles. The court itself has replaced the 'once gently bellied lawn' (185), now torn apart by bulldozers, which have left behind a 'moonscape' (185) of hardened rock. The image combines injured nature, war, and space technology. When Darryl plays singles with Sukie, Sukie revels in an illusion of power, seeing herself as Diana, Isis, Astarte, the embodiments of female strength and grace. But the price of her illusion is the traditional *osculum infame*, the obscene kiss planted on Darryl's nether parts. In the ensuing conversation Darryl complains that modern television has diminished the power of his favourite comic books, by making evil a joke. 'The old comic books, there's real evil there,' he enthuses (190). Benign neo-paganist witchcraft is yielding now to more traditional beliefs. In the hot-tub, the opened roof 'showed early evening's mothering turquoise dome to be an illusion' (191). The witches' conversation in the mansion has also undergone a metamorphosis. They deplore the renaming of Landing Square, and describe their breasts in political terms as 'hemispheres of influence' (195). Alexandra alone begins to perceive uneasily that 'her sustaining ties with nature had slackened' (203), neglecting her garden and abandoning her bubbies. At Darryl's behest, she had graduated to larger statues, constructed from old newspapers on frames of sharp wire, and aimed at the commercial market. For Van Horne they capture

> something in the cultural works now, a sort of end-of-the-party feel. That unreality. Even the clips of the war on TV look unreal, we've all seen too many war movies. (214)

The papier maché images are a fitting correlative to the unreality of Alexandra's inner world and the concomitant separation of powers with which she has collaborated.

The party ends, as far as the witches are concerned, in the final section of the novel, 'Guilt', when Jenny marries Van Horne on Easter Eve. The wedding party exposes both their lack of contact with reality and their childlishness. At the party Alexandra notices new works of art, particularly a female nude in vulnerable position, crouching 'as if to be fucked from behind' (235). The faceless statue is both minimally defined and yet has a quality of 'assaultiveness' (235), its spine resembling the groove for blood in a butcher's block. While Alexandra condemns its 'blasphemous simplification' (235) of female form, she fails to recognise the extent to which she has been guilty of a similar simplification with regard to Jenny. When Jenny appears she removes her bathrobe, with its military chevrons, to reveal a smooth nude body already under assault from cancerous growths. Alexandra is still slow to draw the connections between art and life. She assumes that a second exhibit, a wedding cake, is a fabrication of acrylicked plaster and is disconcerted to discover that it is real. Reality impinges here. Jenny's marriage to Darryl, the result of propinquity under the sunlamps in the laboratory, is characterised, however, quite differently by Jane as the result of nature: 'Naturally nature took its nasty natural course' (239). The ensuing Black Mass, with blasphemous invocations and details of witches' chants and dances drawn from traditional sources, celebrates a Satanic rather than a neo-paganist conception of fertility. Significantly the party ends early. (Jenny has arranged for the scummy hot tub to be drained and treated with fungicide.) As a result Alexandra surprises her babysitter copulating with a local youth. The girl is vulnerably nude, the boy has not even removed his jeans. Alexandra's first reaction is to check on the safety of her virginal daughter, Marcy. Originally Alexandra had been unwilling to attend Darryl's party, refusing to leave her younger children in Marcy's care, on the grounds that 'it's not fair to burden a child with your own responsibilities' (228). While Alexandra fails to extend the moral to herself Updike frames the party scene within the two references, implying that the illusory nurturing of imaginary selves should yield to real responsibilities. In their false nurturing of Jenny, the witches have propelled her into Van Horne's hands.

The remainder of the novel is structured by a series of performances which focus upon the theme of creation, understood in both religious and artistic terms. The witches' actions demonstrate the extent to which their supposed creativity is a misnomer. When Jane Smart plays the second of Bach's suites for unaccompanied cello, a precise correlation exists between music and plot. Bach composed the suite after the death of his wife, Maria, and the marriage of his patron to Princess Henrietta, a woman hostile to Bach. Enclosed in the blackness of night, Jane immerses herself in the music, reaching new heights of solitary proficiency. In the guise of female expression, however, Jane celebrates 'the male voice of death' (284), the mourned death of Maria, the longed for deaths of Henrietta and Jenny. The experience confirms Jane in her solipsism, in the belief that 'the outside of things was sunshine and scatter, the inside of everything was death' (285). Jane's inner musical world is none the less dependent on external technology. In *The Myth of the Machine* Mumford deplored the contemporary separation of art and technics as a modern solecism, and drew attention to the technological complexity of the stringed instrument as an example of a happy reciprocal relation between the aesthetic and the technical.[44] When Jane's Doberman eats her cello, she is condemned to play on the patched up remains, making inferior music entirely for her own consumption, in an ironic demonstration of her reliance on the technology she ostensibly deplores.

The implications are extended in the scene in which the witches hex Jenny by the creation of a wax image. The spell is the result of a false maternal outrage. Jane insists that, in Jenny, 'We've nursed a viper . . . in our bosooms' (226). Ironically, however Jenny is pregnant so that when she dies the event involves the death of both a mother and a child. The spell itself combines traditional recipes for *maleficium* (wax image, pins, the victim's bodily hair) with modern neo-paganism. The act involves the focusing of the image in a mirror while the witches unite their consciousness to project Jenny's identity upon it, thus acting out their belief in the primary of the inner subjective realm. Yet the spell also exploits modern technology. The image is moulded over a Scot-towel, on a Formica counter, and its magic sealed in with aluminium foil. After initial doubts Alexandra elects to cast the spell, because it seems 'simplest, a way of cleaning up another tiny pocket of the world's dirt' (25). The equation between women and dirt is amplified by Jane's gleeful account of the messiness of Jenny's personal habits, revealed in her grubby bathroom, from which Jane gathers the vital ingredients. Military violence is also prominent in the scene. Jane's neglected children figure as an offstage presence, engrossed in television: 'The President was giving speeches only at military installations. The body count was up but so was enemy infiltration' (250). The relevance of the broadcast to the plot of the novel is obvious. By now the body count is up – Ed, Clyde, Felicia, and soon Jenny, whom the witches regard as an enemy infiltrator. Updike counterpoints the two images of violence, inner and outer, as equivalent evils. At the height of the spell 'the television program's violence climaxed' (257), and Jane's hungry children emerge demanding to be fed. Alexandra justifies the casting of the spell on two grounds: aesthetic and natural. She enjoys crafting the image much as she enjoys sculpting her bubbies and using similar tools. Her lack of precise anatomical knowledge makes her, however, an inferior creator: the figure is grossly malformed. The witches defend their spell on the grounds that 'Nature kills constantly and we call her beautiful' (258). After an appeal from Jenny, Alexandra consigns the image to nature, throwing it into a patch of wasteland and willing it gone, 'forgiven by nature's seethe' (269). As her doubts grow, she searches for the image again, confident that she can undo her mischief by carefully reversing the spell, as if running time backwards. The events of the novel, however, undercut her belief in the cyclical nature of time and in the sacredness of nature. The wasteland is described in terms which invite the conception of nature as hostile. Thorns catch at Alexandra's clothes, and insects pullulate in a jungle of festering, struggling plants. When she finds the foil package the wax has been eaten by mites and nothing now remains. The episode enacts a moral, 'In attempting creation we take on creation's burden of guilt, of murder, and irreversibility' (254).

Darryl Van Horne's secular sermon, a rhetorical tour de force entitled 'This is a Terrible Creation', dramatises the concept of nature as evil to exaggerated effect. In his 'Foreword' Updike outlined this approach.

> Man as organism is beset not by 'nothingness' but by predators and parasites themselves obeying the Creator's command to survive and propagate. Disease is a clash of competing vitalities. (*Picked-Up Pieces*, p. 87)

Jenny's image has been reduced to nothingness by predatory parasites. Van Horne's sermon with its subtext of Jenny's approaching death from cancer argues that the evils of human history are as nothing compared to the cruelty inflicted daily in nature. A relentless catalogue follows of disease-bearing insects and bacterial parasites, for all of which man, ostensibly made in the image of God, is only a way-station and breeding place. Darryl describes God in aesthetic terms as a Great Designer, who lavishes his art on the lung flake, the spirochete and the cestode worm, and he therefore urges his audience to 'vote for me next time' (302). The sermon makes a case for, at best, Manichaeanism, at worst, an actively malevolent creator, which the implication that man may as well place his trust in the devil as attempt political or social meliorism.

Updike, however, carefully undercuts the persuasiveness of Darryl's sermon by a preceding sermon from Brenda Parsley, now exercising a female ministry in the Unitarian church. Brenda's congregation is expanding, unlike those of other Eastwick churches, 'their ranks diminished by the summer rebirth of sun worship' (276). In her sermon Brenda appears to reinforce some of the points which the novel has already made. She condemns

> evil wrought in Southeast Asia by fascist politicians and an oppressive capitalism seeking to secure and enlarge its markets for anti-ecological luxuries   (278)

but she also argues that obvious political evils should not blind her flock to the individual responsibility for combating inner evil, nearer to home. She describes creation as inherently good, but insists that evil be recognised for what it is and that psychological, sociological and anthropological mitigations be abjured. While roundly condemning the witches, Brenda none the less uses a feminist rhetoric. She invokes the example of Anne Hutchinson, midwife and mother, as a counter-example to the sexist, world-hating clergy of her day. Brenda, however, is far from being Updike's mouthpiece here, and takes her place in a long line of ineffectual liberal pastors in his fiction. She delivers her sermon in front of a solid brass circle, a sun symbol which has replaced the Christian cross. Her attempt to purvey a watered-down Christianity, with assimilated neo-pagan and feminist trappings, founders on its own inconsistencies. Like Felicia, Brenda has been hexed. A succession of insects, a bee, a moth, a foul-tasting monarch butterfly emerge from her mouth, interrupting the sermon. The insects suggest the connection between Brenda and Darryl: Brenda's confused beliefs have provided Darryl with a platform for his views.

The insect imagery is also, however, applied to Jenny Gabriel, whose thoughts run in tandem with Brenda's sermon. Importantly the knowledge of her impending death has restored to Jenny an awareness of the beauty of nature, lyrically described here in all its seasonal variety. In addition, Jenny now believes that beyond death there stands a 'Great Being'. 'Jenny had come to repose a faith in that Being's custody of her' (279), as opposed to faith in the radiotherapy machines currently fighting for her life. As Jenny watches Brenda, she feels a tense swelling in her body 'as if it were a chrysalis' (281), and eventually bursts into laughter, 'high-voiced, pure, a butterfly of sorts' (281). Traditionally the change from chrysalis to butterfly is a symbol of the passage and release of the human soul. Yet, although Jenny's renewed faith appears to be based on Updike's own neo-orthodox Barthian theology, the novel avoids a blanket espousal of Christianity. Jenny's laughter apparently places Brenda in the camp of the comic devil, but may also suggest Jenny's own inability to take evil seriously. Significantly Jenny is unsure who hexed Brenda. She describes evil as something loosed on the air:

> like those nuclear scientists cooking up the atomic bomb to beat Hitler and Tojo and now so remorseful, like Eisenhower refusing to sign the truce with Ho Chi Minh that would have ended all the trouble, like the late-summer wildflowers, goldenrod and Queen Anne's lace, now loosed from dormant seeds.   (281–2)

The description entertains technological, political and natural acounts of evil which Jenny merely brushes aside as unimportant. The reader, however, can never know whether Jenny's death was a natural event (disease), technologically induced (by X-rays) or the result of active personal evil (the hex), and is left to contemplate the problem.

A final twist is given to the plot with the disappearance of Van Horne, leaving only debts behind. Ironically, given the witches' concern with confidence-building, Van Horne proves to be a confidence-man, a figure with a long pedigree in American literature. The alert reader may already have noticed the mysterious royal prefix, the childhood as infant prodigy, the obscure financial detail and the grandiose schemes, reminiscent of Twain's Mysterious Twins. Like Hawthorne's mesmeric Hollingsworth, Twain's Duke and King, and Melville's Cosmopolitan, Van Horne is a dramatic masquerader and illusionist who runs off in the company of stage-struck Chris Gabriel. The witches' reactions establish both a sliding sale of responses to evil, and the consequences of such responses in terms of artistic creation. For Jane 'there was never anything there. We imagined him' (397). Jane's position is akin to that of the contemporary believer who creates a god by an imaginative leap of faith. Just how flawed that imaginary creation can be emerges in Jane's eventual marriage. Her husband carries her off to a grotesque turreted mansion, stuffed with antique objets d'art, a monument to the cult of the merely aesthetic. Sukie represents both a more Manichaean and a more mechanical position. She seizes upon the possibility that in killing Jenny the witches had been doing Darryl's will, and are therefore absolved. Sukie marries a seller of word-processors, on which she writes paperback romances, deploying standard passions and crises in the calculated production of mechanical fictions. Alexandra, perhaps, reaches a position which mediates aesthetics and technics, inner and outer worlds. For her Darryl is an orthodox devil, inferior to a greater creation:

> He had to improvise on situations others created. . . . He couldn't create. He had no powers of his own that way.   (308)

Alexandra's own creations have been a continual index to her evolution. The grotesque papier maché figures which replaced her bubbies were returned to her with mangled limbs and one thumb torn off, suggesting the tortured witches of old and thus the real direction of Alexandra's inner life. She graduates to an even larger statue, 'big enough for a public space like Kazmierczak Square' (268), as her artistic powers collaborate with the public world. At the close of the novel Alexandra reintegrates inner and outer realms, scaling the statue down to human size and seeing it for what it is – a husband. Her last act of magic is to create that husband. While the feminist reader may scowl at this transformation of witch into wife, the novel does not simply imply that women without husbands go to the devil. Alexandra's last creation asserts the value of her imagination, with certain safeguards. The statue contains both neo-pagan and Christian elements, a pumpkin head, feet modelled on Christ's. Alexandra accepts its sketchiness and imperfection, recognising that up to now her art has been merely primitive and undisciplined. Visiting Providence to buy a cowboy hat for the statue, she takes the opportunity to enrol in formal art classes. There she meets and marries a ceramist from Taos, who takes her west, where 'all the witchcraft belonged to the Hopi and Navajo shamans' (312).

The final words of the novel are given to the unnamed narrator who appears intermittently in the text as the social voice of Eastwick. This figure gives the witches their full due, in terms which reinforce Updike's insistence upon the necessity of a harmonious relation between the imagination and the outer world. The narrator has previously described the witches as monstrous and obscene, but he also notes their importance as 'phantoms in the communal mind' (217) reminding the citizens that there is more to life than their airbrushed advertisements and television commercials. At the end of the novel the years have passed, Kazmierczak Square has become Landing Square once again, and the war is forgotten. The witches, however, are not. They remain in the communal mind as something 'invisible and exciting we do not understand' (316), a reminder of the mystery and density of life. In his 'Foreword' Updike mocked the rationalist for whom the supernatural is an 'intellectual scandal' (*Picked-Up Pieces*, p. 87). The novel ends with the recognition by the narrator that the witches have kept that dimension alive for Eastwick:

it is there when we walk the beach in off-season and the Atlantic

in its blackness mirrors the dense packed gray of the clouds: a
scandal, life like smoke rising twisted into legend.   (316)

The Witches of Eastwick places the Vietnam war in the context of
an extended exploration of the sources of evil, striking a series of
variations on different religious and political explanations. The
responsibility of the technologist is insisted upon, and the 'myth of
the machine' exposed in all its horror. While some elements of the
feminist synthesis are treated satirically, the novel implicitly
argues against the current cultural assignation of sex roles,
whether traditional or exacerbated in recent feminist reaction. In
Updike's analysis it is this sexual polarisation which perpetuates a
double illusion, whether of solipsistic inner life, or of an outer
world of fleshless abstractions. The scandalously fantastic quality
of the novel challenges the reader to resolve that separation both
imaginatively and intellectually.

6
Conclusion

Conclusions, even interim conclusions, which merely summarise and restate preceding arguments, can be tiresome to both reader and writer. Fortunately in this case we can end on a new beginning. Just as this study reached completion, Updike published another novel, *Roger's Version*, which provides a useful opportunity to assess his development. Set in an unnamed New England city before and after Ronald Reagan's second election, the novel offers some surprises, as well as some obvious connections with preceding works, while also, in its intellectual content, furnishing a deliberate mental challenge to the reader. As Updike admitted in interview, cheerfully understating the case,

> I've been accused of writing novels without ideas so I thought I'd write a book with a few ideas in it. (*The Independent*, 15 October 1986, p. 13)

The specific focus of the novel will come as no surprise, however, to readers familiar with Updike's interest in technology and the machine, here interwoven with religious preoccupations. In the opening pages of the novel, Roger Lambert (who gives the reader his subjective, eponymous version of events), an ex-Methodist minister turned Professor of Divinity, encounters Dale Kohler, graduate student and computer buff, who seeks his assistance in obtaining funding for a research project. The nature of this project – to reveal the existence of God by employing a computer – strikes a modern variant on the Argument from Design, and combines art, religion and technology in a fashion highly reminiscent of previous novels. The belief in the machine as a pathway to salvation, common to *Rabbit Redux* and *The Witches of Eastwick*, is accompanied by a parallel faith in the powers of art. Dale's project involves the use of computer graphics, by means of which he intends to produce a pictorial representation of the deity on his computer screen. Where Dale's frequent expositions of his project, and its sources in cosmology and astrophysics, recall George Caldwell's science lesson (expanded here to reader satiation point) he also shares with Peter Caldwell the expectation that art will provide a transcendent revelation. Roger's horror at Dale's implicit notion of a deducible God, to be revealed by the machine, is couched in familiar Kierkegaardian terms. He finds the whole idea

> aesthetically and ethically repulsive. Aesthetically because it describes a God Who lets Himself be intellectually trapped, and ethically because it eliminates faith from religion, it takes away our freedom to believe or doubt. (23)

The appearance of Dale from the mental world of 'clean' technology is not, however, the only factor to disturb Roger's stable state. Dale also initiates contact between Roger and his niece Verna, mother of illegitimate Paula, and an inhabitant of a project of a different kind – a messy slum. Roger's attraction to Verna, which runs in tandem with Dale's affair with Roger's wife Esther, takes the reader into a familiar dualism of flesh and spirit, physical chaos and mental order, already explored in *The Witches of Eastwick* and *A Month of Sundays*. Indeed, in his asides, footnotes, imagined re-creations, glosses and etymologies, Roger is as self-conscious a narrator as Thomas Marshfield, though in this reworking of *The Scarlet Letter* (as Updike indicated in the *Independent* interview) the tale is told from the point of view of the betrayed husband. Just as Marshfield drew on specialised knowledge of theology, so Roger, whose particular field of expertise is the heresies of the Early Church, batters the reader with abstruse speculations, gradually evolving a defence of the flesh somewhat similar to Marshfield's adulterous apologetics. Where Roger's Latin, Greek and Hebrew bolster his belief in the necessity of a conjunction between flesh and spirit, Dale's computer language (its symbols faithfully reproduced in darker typography (227)) invokes a world of overarching mind, and is almost equally inaccessible to the general reader. Roger's disnumerate son, Richie, appears to be included in the novel so that Dale can explain the functioning of the binary system and the basics of computer programming to him, and thus to the reader.

Importantly, however, the themes of the novel are firmly connected to its narrative strategies. Updike structures the novel in a fashion to call attention to the computational and the mechanical, just as, in *Rabbit Redux*, McLuhanite messages were inscribed within the fictional medium. Rather than being provided with titles, the five chapters are simply headed 'One', 'Two' and so on, and are subdivided into sections introduced by Roman numerals (the number of these sections varies significantly, as we shall see).

The protagonists of the central quartet are also characterised in mathematical terms, in what is certainly Updike's most overt employment of the collective protagonist. Dale, the computer expert, is drawn to Esther, also an expert mathematician, who is described as thinking 'like an accountant' (246). Esther's concern with her own figure (she weighs exactly 'one oh oh' pounds (165), and starves herself whenever the scales tip 100) aligns her with Dale's binary heaven. Verna and Roger, messily fleshy, also eventually combine, as Roger evolves from an initial coolness to a renewed involvement with the chaos and contingency of existence. In the early pages Roger registers the boredom of his marriage and the staleness of his faith, commenting wryly that in giving up the ministry he had progressed from 'distribution' to 'quality control' (61). The mechanical nature of his present life is highlighted in his memories of his over-emotionally 'messy' family in Ohio, whence he has fled to a cooler existence in the East, and in his mental habits. (At one point he methodically lists his reactions to Dale in sequence from a) to f).) Updike's own distaste for the academicisation and institutionalisation of religion is brought out in the scene in which the members of the Grants Committee interview Dale. Initially the members of the panel view Dale's application with disfavour. When, however, Roger intervenes to express his hostility to any notion of a God who is other than *totaliter aliter* (unknowable), his ecumenical, liberal colleagues cannot bear to be aligned with his Barthian neo-orthodoxy and agree to award a grant. In computer terms, Roger's negative input converts the panel to agreement. Just as Dale takes money from the university to support his project, so Verna benefits from a series of transactions with Roger (money for study, for an abortion, for a plane ticket) which support her in hers. Figures are substituted for human interaction in both cases, as Roger oscillates between the two sides of the central polarity.

An early scene establishes the parallel between the central quartet and the opposed, dualistic worlds of mind and flesh. At a Thanksgiving dinner, Dale instructs the hapless Richie in the binary system on which his programming depends, explaining the function of logic states in the computer. Drawing three boxes, enclosing the three words AND, OR, NOT, he expounds the system to his bemused onlookers:

'a current and no current, a one and a zero in terms of the binary code, will give a hot output from the OR and not from the AND, but if the AND output then goes into a NOT it comes out –'
'Hot,' Verna said.   (106)

Continuing his exposition Dale feeds four four-bit numbers in sequence into his hypothetical gates to produce 'oh one one one' (from the OR circuit), 'oh oh oh one' (from the AND circuit) and (when the OR circuit is linked to a NOT) 'one oh oh oh'. Readers who empathise with Richie's confusions at this point should bear in mind the following simple ground rules.

a) If all inputs to the AND are 1, output is 1. If any input is 0, output is 0. (Everything must be true.)

b) If any input to the OR is 1, output is 1. Only if all inputs are 0 is output 0. (Only one thing needs to be true.)

c) If input to NOT is 1, output is 0. If input is 0, output is 1. (Negativisation.)

Though the subtleties of the OR, AND, and NOT gates are somewhat beyond the scope of this study they are clearly an operating factor in Updike's novel, particularly in its numerical structure. Chapters One and Two each contain three sections, which progress from Dale (I) to the Lamberts (II) and to Verna (III) dramatising the opposition of Dale and Verna in a structural alternation. As events evolve, Chapter Three (also three sections) intermeshes the experiences of all four characters, to be followed in Four by two sections which oppose Dale (I) and Verna (II) once more, and thence in Chapter Five by four sections as the foursome disentangle themselves.

In the Thanksgiving scene, the erotic permutations of the quartet are anticipated in binary and computer imagery. Dale has extolled computer graphics (112), particularly their capacity for handling a wealth of visual information in figures. He is considerably taken by Esther's figure which is presented in electronic terms:

> the effect was of sudden living color, of a tuning adjustment on the UHF channel . . . . her green velvet shimmering . . . her gingery hair glistening in a multitude of bright points . . . her prominent eyes processing irony and flirtation with electronic rapidity. . . . The aura of boredom was tuned out.   (121)

The preceding discussion of hot and cold currents informs the human scene in which the two pairs re-form, their currents turned on in an erotic sense. When Esther divides the Thanksgiving pies, her offer of a portion is readily translatable into erotic terms. Given the choice of pumpkin or apple, Dale asks for 'a little bit' of both. Their subsequent exchanges rely on double entendre:

> 'A *little* bit? Not enough to make a byte?'
> 'No, that wouldn't leave any for anybody else. A byte is usually eight bits.'
> 'One of each.' She handed him his plate. 'Does that make an OR or an AND?'
> 'If one of them wasn't there and that made the one next to it disappear, that would be an AND.'   (119)

While the mathematicians pair off, Verna and Roger disappear to the messy kitchen and make physical contact over the garbage pail. The cold hostility of Roger and Esther, the equal coolness between Dale and Verna (neither of whom is 'turned on' by the other) yield to two different dualities, realigned in hot agreement. The scene invites a playful assignation of values in binary terms, with Esther and Dale as 1 (mind), Roger and Verna as 0 (flesh). In their original conjunction Roger and Esther represented a union of flesh and mind: 1 + 0 as input to an AND gate, resulting in 0, the triumph of the flesh which they enjoyed in their early illicit courtship. As their relationship converts into hostility, their input passes through an OR gate, leading to a domination of 1 (the mind) and eventually passing Esther over to Dale. Though the two new pairs seem initially productive, subsequent events reveal the inadequacy of one dimensional pairings. The agreement of Dale and Esther eventually reveals the deficiencies of the mind, while that of Roger and Verna has equally troubling consequences in the world of the flesh, until at the end the two pairs re-form (as 1 + 0 in each case) in a necessary conjunction of flesh and spirit. The crisis for each couple comes in Chapter Four in which Dale's recognition of the necessity of the flesh is immediately followed by Verna's opposed recognition of its weaknesses.

Throughout the novel Dale's erotic activities with Esther are described in excessive length and detail. On the one hand, as these scenes are relayed to the reader through Roger's obsessively fleshly imagination, the excessive physical detail serves to underline the one-dimensional quality of his viewpoint. The descriptions, however, also direct irony at Dale. Dale is initially delighted by Esther's worship of his phallus, which now takes on independent existence, separate from his own mind.

> He feels, erect, split into two creatures, of whom the much smaller has much the greater share of vitality, even of spirituality. (230)

Spirit and body, however, are not so easily divided as puritan Dale would like, and his initial pleasure yields to an uneasy awareness of the mechanical nature of their couplings. Just as a computer handles infinite input through its gates, in an endlessly repeated sequence of mechanical operations, so with Esther

> it all becomes a matter of mouths, openings interlocking and contorted like the apertures and intersections of hyperspace. (225)

Exploiting every possible aperture and 'portal' (133) Dale feels 'caught up in an abnormal geometry' (225), until eventually his body 'protested its mechanical role as her partner in these feats' (230), responding by switching off into impotence. In addition Dale is repelled by his impression that Esther's contortions reveal an 'exhibitionist defiance' (231), as if she were 'showing' some third party, reducing Dale merely to a figure in 'an ongoing transaction' (231). The immersion in the flesh, however, does have some productive results. In Chapter Four Dale's memories of Esther interrupt him at the computer. Before the memories he seeks in vain for evidence of the Creator in the strings of figures produced by the machine. Proceeding without a precise programme, trusting to intuition, he drifts into erotic reminiscence and suddenly 'sees' a face, and a hand on his computer screen. (The suggestion of the fleshly Incarnation is unavoidable.) When, however, he types 'repeat', the screen goes blank, and he is left to the recognition that 'Zero is information also' (243). The fleeting vision is not amenable to mechanist control. Chapter Four may thus be envisaged as an OR gate. In section I mind is reduced to zero, and in section II the flesh is also revealed as insufficient.

In section II Verna is the focus. Throughout the novel Verna has revelled almost embarrassingly in the flesh. Like Dale, she also sees herself as a creative duality, though in her case the fleshly appendage is Paula. Verna had enjoyed her pregnancy because of 'that incredible thing of being split and there suddenly being two of you' (178), of creating apparently out of her own flesh. When she becomes pregnant again, however, she accedes to Roger's advice to have an abortion. (The event is clearly designed to highlight the moral problems inherent in envisaging the human being as flesh rather than spirit.) Roger also sees the abortion in terms of human mathematics here. The foetus is aborted in order to preserve the security of Paula and of Verna, herself not much more than a child. 'I was killing an unborn child, to try to preserve a born one. Two born ones' (213). This easy accountancy, however, in which a subtraction is presented as a gain, is speedily exposed in Verna's flippant comment, 'One down, and one to go' (218), glancing at Paula as she leaves the clinic. The phrase prefigures the near disaster in Four, II, in which Verna batters her child. Verna's obsession with the flesh proves as dehumanising to Paula as Esther's mental couplings are to Dale. Both have left a vital factor out of account. Her leg broken, Paula is described in mechanical imagery, lying unnaturally still, 'like a person with a Walkman singing in her ears' (251), her cries of pain 'like the grinding of a non-starting engine that has drained its battery' (253). In her plaster cast her toes resemble 'a row of round digits, [which] seemed a fragment left over from some visual collision or subtraction' (259). Where Dale's experiences in the computer building revealed the importance of the flesh, the treatment of Paula in the hi-tech hospital reasserts a necessary order. When Roger is questioned as to the circumstances of Paula's injury, he lies to protect Verna but is immediately caught out. Though the doctor tells him that 'we appreciate your input' (258), he none the less decides to keep Paula in for observation. Verna's flirtatious antics also fail. Though 'an electricity had been set up' (258) between Verna and the doctor, it is not sufficient to override his decision. Roger's verdict points to the inadequacy of Verna's solipsistic belief in her own powers as Paula's creator:

> the tribe used to raise the children once the young mother had them. There was an overall program and everybody shared it. Now there is no tribe. There is no overall program.   (268)

Though Verna's messy immersion in the flesh has led to actual violence and near disaster, Roger points out that she should not accuse herself too harshly: 'according to the Bible, what looks like a mess may be just right really, and people that look very fine and smooth and shiny from the outside are really the lost ones' (269). The false dualism of flesh and spirit yields to the recognition that 'Not either/or but both/and lies at the heart of the cosmos' (270).

The binary opposition of Dale and Verna is followed in Five by four sections, which amplify the message. In the first the tribe re-emerges and the overall social program reasserts itself, as the DSS step in to protect Paula, assigning part-guardianship of her to the Lamberts. In the second section, Myron Kriegman explodes Dale's arguments from design. Firstly Myron points out that Dale's theories rely on the notion of a unitary universe. There may however be more than one (289), even a multiplicity of created worlds, to which the dualism of the binary system is inappropriate. When Dale describes quarks as dual, carrying positive or negative charges, Myron pounces. 'They invariably occur in threes and cannot be pried apart' (291). For Myron that fact suggests the three dimensions of space. 'Now, let's ask ourselves, what's so hot about three dimensions? Why don't we exist in two or four or twenty-four?' (291). Answering his own question he points out that only in three dimensions can an indissoluble knot be formed, using the fourth dimension of time.

> Space-time. Three spatial dimensions, plus time. It knots. It freezes. The seed of the universe has come into being.   (292)

When Myron argues that in terms of dimensions, 'Four is plenty', Dale nods, 'thinking of Esther and myself, himself and Verna' (292), highlighting the parallel with the quartet's successive

combinations. (For the reader the significance of the four sections
of Five also leaps into prominence.) When Dale objects that all
this talk of 'seed' is only metaphor, Myron exults, 'What isn't?'
(293). Metaphor allows ambiguities and paradoxes to coexist, in a
fashion which argues against polarisation. Language may convey
both/and rather than either/or, as a word may mean two or more
things simultaneously, as a project may be a mental plan or a
messy slum. Indeed, Kriegman's subsequent exposition of the
origins of life in crystal formation in fine clays could provide Dale
with an opening. As one of Roger's colleagues pointed out (201)
Adam means 'clay' or 'red earth' just as Eve (Hawwah) means
'life'. Threes might also suggest the indissoluble trinity of spirit,
deity and flesh. Dale, however, is too much of a mechanist to size
upon these metaphoric possibilities and remains lost in the world
of either/or.

In the third section, Verna and Roger's last meeting takes place
in an emblematic locale, an expensive restaurant, situated on top
of the city's highest skyscraper, called the 360, because it turns
through one complete revolution every one-and-a-half hours.
Slowly moving through three dimensions, Roger decides not to
pursue his affair with Verna. Respect for time is a factor here.
Roger excuses Esther's infidelities as a product of her awareness of
time running out for her, and concludes that 'Esther is part of my
life. . . . I'm too old to do any more rearranging' (31). His
marriage will remain an indissoluble knot. At the close of the
scene, having agreed to buy Verna a ticket home, Roger uses an
automatic cash teller. The machine flashes up a message:

DO YOU WISH ANY MORE TRANSACTIONS?
I punched the NO button. (312)

An irony remains however. In the fourth section Roger returns
to his 'self-satisfying loops of theology' (313) (mechanical
operations analogous to computer loops) but is continually
disturbed by the presence of Paula. In addition there is a strong
hint that another new factor is about to interrupt the regained
equilibrium. Earlier, when making love with Dale, Esther had left
her diaphragm out of her calculations, deciding to gamble. Now
she has become irritable and abstracted, eating more and sleeping
late (all the symptoms of Ruth's pregnancy in *Rabbit, Run*). In
addition she has stopped watching her weight and now weighs

more than 100 pounds (316). The novel closes with a teasing exchange, in which Roger hears in Esther's 'rounded' voice 'an amused glint, a hint or seed' (316). Roger's return to the status quo may yet be disturbed by a fresh evolutionary development, and the novel therefore ends, like *Of the Farm*, on a productive linguistic ambiguity. New possibilities are on the horizon. In the *Independent* interview Updike indicated that he plans to retell *The Scarlet Letter* once more, from the point of view of the woman (Hester, Esther) as opposed to the adulterer (Marshfield, Dimmesdale, Dale) or the betrayed spouse (Jane Chillingworth, Roger Chillingworth, Roger Lambert.) The novel therefore remains only one 'version' in an anticipated intertextual trilogy which will rework the past fiction through all its possible dimensions. *Roger's Version* thus teaches its readers to move outside polarity and to embrace the indeterminacy of existence, opening up fresh lines of enquiry rather than closing them off. In its open-ended closure it seems a peculiarly appropriate point on which to conclude this study.

Notes

1. See Michiko Kakutani's 1981 interview, which quotes Podhoretz and Mailer.

2. J. A. Ward, 'John Updike's Fiction', *Critique*, 5, 1 (1962), 27–40.

3. Joseph Epstein, 'John Updike: Promises, Promises', *Commentary*, 75, 1 (1983), p. 55.

4. Quoted in David McCullough, 'Eye on Books', *Book of the Month Club News*, July 1974, p. 7.

5. Reported by Ann-Janine Morey, *Christian Century*, 20 November 1985.

6. Yves le Pellec, 'Rabbit Underground', in *Les Américanistes: New French Criticism on Modern American Fiction*, ed. Ira D. and Christiane Johnson, Port Washington: Kennikat Press, 1978, 94–109.

7. Inna Levidova, 'John Updike's *The Centaur* in Russia', *Soviet Literature*, 10 (1965), 188–94.

8. Biographical information derives from interviews listed in the bibliography, and from Jane Howard, 'Can a Nice Novelist Finish First?', *Life*, 4 November 1966, 74–82.

9. All page references are to the hardback (Deutsch) edition, followed, where pagination differs, by their equivalents in Penguin paperback.

10. Updike appears to be influenced here by the writings of Lewis Mumford, whom I paraphrase at this point: *The Conduct of Life* (London: Secker and Warburg, 1952, pp. 178–9). Mumford's discussion of technology is relevant to *The Witches of Eastwick*, and his analysis of suburbia as the realm of play and the pleasure principle informs *Couples: The City in History* (London: Secker and Warburg, 1961, pp. 494–6). In his essay 'Quarters for an Aging Population' (1956) reproduced in *The Urban Prospect* (London: Secker and Warburg, 1968) Mumford attacks the segregation of the old in communities where their only occupation is remaining alive. Updike refers to Mumford in *Hugging the Shore*, p. 104.

11. See Norman O. Brown, *Life Against Death* (London: Routledge and Kegan Paul, 1959); Erich Fromm, *The Sane Society* (London: Routledge and Kegan Paul, 1959); Herbert Marcuse, *Eros and Civilization* (Boston: Beacon Press, 1955); and William H. Whyte, *The Organization Man* (New York: Simon and Schuster, 1956).

12. Howard interview, p. 82.

13. Gerry Brenner, '*Rabbit Run*: John Updike's Criticism of the "Return to Nature"', *Twentieth Century Literature*, XII (1966), 3–14, an exceptionally important essay.

14. Howard interview, p. 74C.

15. A connection acknowledged by Updike, in interview with Charlie Reilly, p. 158.

16. Marshall McLuhan, *The Mechanical Bride* (Boston: Beacon Paperback, 1951); *The Gutenberg Galaxy* (London: Routledge and Kegan Paul, 1962); *Understanding Media* (London: Routledge and Kegan Paul, 1964); *The Medium is the Message* (New York: Bantam, 1967); Marshall McLuhan and Quentin Fiore, *War and Peace in the Global Village* (New York: Bantam, 1968). Useful discussions of McLuhan include Barry Day, *The Message of Marshall McLuhan* (London: Lintas, 1967); Gerald E. Stern (ed.), *McLuhan: Hot and Cool* (London: Penguin, 1967); Tony Tanner, *City of Words* (London: Cape, 1971); Jonathan Miller, *McLuhan* (London: Fontana, 1971); John Fekete, *The Critical Twilight* (London: Routledge and Kegan Paul, 1978); and Christopher Brookeman, *American Culture and Society Since the 1930s* (London: Macmillan, 1984).

17. Readers are referred for a fuller discussion to Ernest Bornemann, *The Psychoanalysis of Money* (New York: Urizen Books, 1976).

18. *First Person: Conversations on Writers and Writing*, preface by Frank Gado (Schenectady: Union Press, 1973) p. 89.

19. A. G. George, *The First Sphere: A Study of Kierkegaardian Aesthetics* (London: Asia, 1965), provides a succinct account.

20. Reilly interview, p. 160.

21. Two critics have drawn attention to this emphasis on art and perception: Elizabeth Tallent, op. cit., p. 42, and Dee Birch Cameron, 'The Unitarian Wife And The One-Eyed Man', *Ball State University Forum*, 21, iii (1980), 54–64.

22. Reilly interview, p. 174.

23. The novel has, however, attracted some excellent critical readings, the best of which are informed by recent French critical theory: Robert Detweiler, 'Updike's *A Month of Sundays* and The Language of the Unconscious', *Journal of the American Academy of Religion*, XLVII, 4 (1979), 609–25; Terrence A. Doody, 'Updike's Idea of Reification', *Contemporary Literature*, XX, 2 (1979), 204–20, and John T. Matthews, 'The Word as Scandal: Updike's *A Month of Sundays*', *Arizona Quarterly*, 39, 4 (1983), 351–80.

24. Reilly interview, p. 168.

25. Reilly interview, p. 156.

26. A point developed in *The Witches of Eastwick*. See below.

27. Matthews, p. 356.

28. Kathleen Lathrop's article is cited in the bibliography. Barry Amis's remarks, in an unpublished paper, are quoted in Joyce Markle, '*The Coup*: Illusions and Insubstantial Impressions', in William R. Macnaughton (ed.), *Critical Essays on John Updike* (Boston: Hall, 1982). A perceptive discussion of *The Coup* also figures in Donald J. Greiner, *John Updike's Novels* (Athens: Ohio University Press, 1984).

29. William Findlay, 'Interview with John Updike', *Cencrastus*, 15 (1984), p. 34.

30. Reilly interview, p. 156.

31. Basil Davidson, *Old Africa Rediscovered* (London: Gollancz, 1959), p. 57. Readers who wish to pursue the historical sources for Kush should consult the list provided in the novel itself.

32. Limitations of space proscribe a full bibliography. The following recent

works are of primary importance: Andrew M. Greeley, *The Persistence of Religion* (London: SCM Press, 1973); Lauran Paine, *Witches in Fact and Fantasy* (London: Robert Hale, 1971); Doreen Valiente, *An ABC of Witchcraft Past and Present* (London: Robert Hale, 1973); Starhawk, *The Spiral Dome* (San Francisco: Harper and Row, 1979); Charles A. Hoyt, *Witchcraft* (Carbondale: South Illinois University Press, 1981); Pennethorne Hughes, *Witchcraft* (London: Longmans, Green, 1952).

33. Jeffrey B. Russell, *A History of Witchcraft* (London: Thames and Hudson, 1980).

34. Margaret Murray, *The Witch Cult in Western Europe* (Oxford: Clarendon, 1921).

35. Norman Cohn, *Europe's Inner Demons* (London: Paladin, 1976).

36. Naomi R. Goldenberg, *Changing of the Gods: Feminism and the end of traditional religions* (Boston: Beacon Press, 1979).

37. Erica Jong, *Witches* (London: Granada, 1981).

38. Rosemary Radford Ruether, *To Change the World: Christology and Cultural Criticism* (London: SCM Press, 1981).

39. Brian Easlea, *Witch Hunting, Magic and the New Philosophy* (Brighton: Harvester, 1984).

40. Lewis Mumford, *The Myth of the Machine: Technics and Human Development* (London: Secker and Warburg, 1967) and *The Pentagon of Power* (New York: Harcourt Brace Jovanovich, 1970).

41. Dorothy Dinnerstein, *The Mermaid and the Minotaur* (New York: Harper and Row, 1976).

42. Barbara Ehrenreich and Deirdre English, *Witches, Midwives and Nurses* (London: Compendium, 1974).

43. *The Myth of the Machine*, pp. 171–2.

44. *The Myth of the Machine*, p. 254. Jane's comments (p. 209) on the connections between pyramids and the cult of death are also drawn from Mumford's analysis of the Pyramid Age.

Select Bibliography

MAJOR WORKS BY JOHN UPDIKE

Novels
The Poorhouse Fair (New York: Knopf, and London: Gollancz, 1959).
Rabbit, Run (New York, Knopf, 1960; London: Deutsch, 1961).
The Centaur (New York: Knopf, and London: Deutsch, 1963).
Of the Farm (New York: Knopf, 1965; London: Deutsch, 1966).
Couples (New York: Knopf, and London: Deutsch, 1968).
Rabbit Redux (New York: Knopf, 1971; London: Deutsch, 1972).
A Month of Sundays (New York: Knopf, and London: Deutsch, 1975).
Marry Me: A Romance (New York: Knopf, 1976; London: Deutsch, 1977).
The Coup (New York: Knopf, 1978; London: Deutsch, 1979).
Rabbit Is Rich (New York: Knopf, 1981; London: Deutsch, 1982).
The Witches of Eastwick (New York: Knopf, and London: Deutsch, 1984).
Roger's Version (New York: Knopf, and London: Deutsch, 1986).

Short Story Collections
The Same Door (New York: Knopf, 1959; London: Deutsch, 1962).
Pigeon Feathers and Other Stories (New York: Knopf, and London: Deutsch, 1962).
Olinger Stories: A Selection (New York: Knopf, 1964).
The Music School (New York: Knopf, 1966; London: Deutsch, 1967).
Bech: A Book (New York, Knopf, and London: Deutsch, 1970).
Museums and Women and Other Stories (New York: Knopf, 1972; London: Deutsch, 1973).
Too Far to Go: The Maples Stories (New York: Fawcett, 1979), and as *Your Lover Just Called: Stories of Joan and Richard Maple* (London: Penguin, 1980).
Problems and Other Stories (New York: Knopf, 1979; London: Deutsch, 1980).
Bech is Back (New York: Knopf, 1982; London: Deutsch, 1983).

Drama
Three Texts from Early Ipswich: A Pageant (Ipswich, Massachusetts: 17th Century Day Committee, 1968).
Buchanan Dying (New York: Knopf, and London: Deutsch, 1974).

Verse
The Carpentered Hen and Other Tame Creatures (New York: Harper, 1958) and as *Hoping for a Hoopoe* (London: Gollancz, 1959).
Telephone Poles and Other Poems (New York: Knopf, and London: Deutsch, 1963).

Verse (New York: Fawcett, 1965).

Dog's Death (Cambridge, Massachusetts: Lowell House, 1965).

The Angels (Pensacola, Florida: King and Queen Press, 1968).

Bath after Sailing (Monroe, Connecticut: Pendulum Press, 1968).

Midpoint and Other Poems (New York: Knopf, and London: Deutsch, 1969).

Seventy Poems (London: Penguin, 1972).

Six Poems (New York: Aloe, 1973).

Query (New York: Albondocani Press, 1974).

Cunts (Upon Receiving the Swingers Life Club Membership Solicitation) (New York: Hallman, 1974).

Tossing and Turning (New York: Knopf, and London: Deutsch, 1977).

Sixteen Sonnets (Cambridge, Massachusetts: Halty Ferguson, 1979).

An Oddly Lovely Day Alone (Richmond, Virginia: Waves Press, 1979).

Five Poems (Cleveland: Bits Press, 1980).

Jester's Dozen (Northridge, California: Lord John Press, 1984).

Facing Nature (New York: Knopf, 1985; London: Deutsch, 1986).

Prose

Assorted Prose (New York: Knopf, and London: Deutsch, 1965).

Picked-Up Pieces (New York: Knopf, 1975; London: Deutsch, 1976).

Hugging the Shore: Essays and Criticism (New York: Knopf, 1983; London: Deutsch, 1984).

Manuscript Collection: Harvard University, Cambridge, Massachusetts.

Interviews

Atlas, James, 'John Updike Breaks Out Of Suburbia', *New York Times Magazine*, 10 December 1978, pp. 60–76.

Boyers, Robert *et al*, 'An Evening with John Updike', *Salmagundi*, 57 (1982), 42–56.

Findlay, William, 'Interview with John Updike', *Cencrastus*, 15 (1984), 30–6.

Gado, Frank, 'A Conversation with John Updike', *The Idol*, 47 (1971), 3–32.

Kakutani, Michiko, 'Turning Sex and Guilt Into an American Epic', *Saturday Review*, October 1981, 14–22.

Reilly, Charlie, 'A Conversation with John Updike', *Canto 3*, 3 (1980), 148–78.

Rubins, Josh, 'The Industrious Drifter in Room Two', *Harvard Magazine*, 76 (1974), 42–5, 51.

Samuels, Charles T., 'The Art of Fiction XLIII: John Updike', *Paris Review*, 45 (1968), 85–117.

Seib, Philip, 'A Lovely Way Through Life: An Interview with John Updike', *Southwest Review*, 66, 4 (1981), 341–50.

SECONDARY CRITICISM

Bibliography

Gearhart, Elizabeth A., *John Updike: A Comprehensive Bibliography with Selected Annotations* (Norwood, Pennsylvania: Norwood Editions, 1978).

Olivas, Michael A., *An Annotated Bibliography of John Updike Criticism 1967–1973, and a Checklist of His Works* (New York: Garland, 1975).

Sokoloff, B. A. and Posner, Mark E., *John Updike: A Comprehensive Bibliography* (Norwood, Pennyslvania: Norwood Editions, 1973).

Taylor, C. Clarke, *John Updike: A Bibliography* (Kent, Ohio: Kent State University Press, 1968).

Critical Studies

Burchard, Rachael C., *John Updike: Yea Sayings* (Carbondale: Southern Illinois University Press, 1971).

Detweiler, Robert, *John Updike* (New York: Twayne, 1972; revised edition, 1984).

Greiner, Donald J., *The Other John Updike: Poems/Short Stories/Prose/Play* (Athens: Ohio University Press, 1981).

Greiner, Donald J., *John Updike's Novels* (Athens: Ohio University Press, 1984).

Greiner, Donald J., *Adultery in the American Novel: Updike, James and Hawthorne* (Columbia: University of South Carolina Press, 1985).

Hamilton, Alice and Kenneth, *The Elements of John Updike* (Grand Rapids, Michigan: Eerdmans, 1970).

Hunt, George W., S.J., *John Updike and the three great secret things: Sex, Religion and Art* (Grand Rapids, Michigan: Eerdmans, 1980).

Macnaughton, William R. (ed.), *Critical Essays on John Updike* (Boston: Hall, 1982).

Markle, Joyce B., *Fighters and Lovers: Theme in the Novels of John Updike* (New York: New York University Press, 1973).

Samuels, Charles T., *John Updike* (Minneapolis: University of Minnesota Press, 1969).

Searles, George J., *The Fiction of Philip Roth and John Updike* (Carbondale: Southern Illinois University Press, 1985).

Tallent, Elizabeth, *Married Men and Magic Tricks: John Updike's Erotic Heroes* (Berkeley: Creative Arts, 1982).

Taylor, Larry E., *Pastoral and Anti-Pastoral Elements in John Updike's Fiction* (Carbondale: Southern Illinois University Press, 1971).

Thorburn, David and Eiland, Howard (ed.), *John Updike: A Collection of Critical Essays* (Englewood Cliffs, New Jersey: Prentice Hall, 1979).

Uphaus, Suzanne H., *John Updike* (New York: Ungar, 1980).

Vargo, Edward P., *Rainstorms and Fire: Ritual in the Novels of John Updike* (Port Washington, New York: Kennikat Press, 1973).

Vaughan, Philip H., *John Updike's Images of America* (Reseda, California: Mojave, 1981).

Critical Articles and Chapters in Books

Alley, Alvin D., '*The Centaur*: Transcendental Imagination and Metaphoric Death', *English Journal*, 56 (1967), 982–5.

Berryman, Charles, 'Updike and Contemporary Witchcraft', *South Atlantic Quarterly*, 85, 1 (1986), 1–9.

Cameron, Dee Birch, 'The Unitarian Wife and The One-Eyed Man: Updike's *Marry Me* and "Sunday Teasing",' *Ball State University Forum*, 21, iii (1980), 54–64.

Chukwu, Augustine, 'The Dreamer as Leader: Ellelloû in John Updike's *The Coup*', *Literary Half-Yearly*, 23, 1 (1982), 61–9.

Detweiler, Robert, 'Updike's *A Month of Sundays* and the Language of the

Unconscious', *Journal of the American Academy of Religion*, XLVII, 4 (1979), 609–25.

Doody, Terrence A., 'Updike's Idea of Reification', *Contemporary Literature*, 20 (1979), 204–20.

Eiland, Howard, 'Updike's Womanly Man', *Centennial Review*, 26, 4 (1982), 312–23.

Galloway, David D., 'The Absurd Man as Saint: The Novels of John Updike', *Modern Fiction Studies*, 11 (1964), 111–27.

Hallissy, Margaret, 'Marriage, Morality and Maturity in Updike's *Marry Me*,' *Renascence*, XXXVII, 2 (1985), 96–107.

Harper, Howard M., *Desperate Faith: A Study of Bellow, Salinger, Mailer, Baldwin and Updike* (Chapel Hill: University of North Carolina Press, 1967, pp. 162–90).

Lathrop, Kathleen, '*The Coup*: John Updike's Modernist Masterpiece', *Modern Fiction Studies*, 31, 2 (1985), 249–62.

Matthews, John T., 'The Word as Scandal: Updike's *A Month of Sundays*', *Arizona Quarterly*, 39, 4 (1983), 351–80.

Modern Fiction Studies, 20, 1 (1974). John Updike Special Issue.

Moore, Jack B., 'Africa Under Western Eyes: Updike's *The Coup* and Other Fantasies', *African Literature Today*, 14 (1984), 60–7.

Myers, David, 'The Questing Fear: Christian Allegory in John Updike's *The Centaur*', *Twentieth Century Literature*, 17 (1971), 73–82.

Plagman, Linda M., 'Eros and Agape: The Opposition in Updike's *Couples*', *Renascence*, 28 (1976), 83–93.

Rupp, Richard H., 'John Updike: Style in Search of a Center', *Sewanee Review*, 75 (1967), 693–709.

Stubbs, John C., 'The Search for Perfection in *Rabbit, Run*', *Critique*, 10, 2 (1968), 94–101.

Tanner, Tony, *City of Words: American Fiction 1950–70* (London: Cape, 1971, pp. 273–94).

Vanderwerken, David L., 'Rabbit 'Re-docks': Updike's Inner Space Odyssey', *College Literature*, 2 (1975), 73–8.

Waller, Gary, 'Updike's *Couples*: A Barthian Parable', *Research Studies*, 40 (1972), 10–21.

Ward, J. A., 'John Updike's Fiction', *Critique*, 5, 1 (1962), 27–40.

Zylstra, S. A., 'John Updike and the Parabolic Nature of the World', *Soundings*, 56 (1973), 323–37.

Index